LIGHT FOR THE JOURNEY THROUGH DRY BONE VALLEY

How Points of Connection in You, Your Relationships, and Your Community Can Reinvigorate Your Life

Patricia Boyce

Copyright © 2023 by **Patricia Boyce**

All rights reserved. No part of this publication may be reproduced, distributed, or transmitted in any form or by any means, without prior written permission.

Scripture quotations marked (ESV) are taken from the ESV® Bible (The Holy Bible, English Standard Version®). ESV® Text Edition: 2016. Copyright © 2001 by Crossway, a publishing ministry of Good News Publishers. The ESV® text has been reproduced in cooperation with and by permission of Good News Publishers. Unauthorized reproduction of this publication is prohibited. Used by permission. All rights reserved.

Scripture quotations marked (NASB) are taken from the (NASB®) New American Standard Bible®, Copyright © 1960, 1971, 1977, 1995, 2020 by The Lockman Foundation. Used by permission. All rights reserved. www.Lockman.org.

Scripture quotations marked (NIV) are taken from the Holy Bible, New International Version®, NIV® Copyright © 1973, 1978, 1984, 2011 by Biblica, Inc.® Used by permission. All rights reserved worldwide.

Scripture quotations marked (NKJV) are taken from the New King James Version®. Copyright © 1982 by Thomas Nelson, Inc. Used by permission. All rights reserved.

Scripture quotations marked (NLT) are taken from the Holy Bible, New Living Translation (NLT), copyright © 1996, 2004, 2015 by Tyndale House Foundation. Used by permission of Tyndale House Publishers, Inc., Carol Stream, Illinois 60188. All rights reserved.

Renown Publishing
www.renownpublishing.com

Light for the Journey Through Dry Bone Valley / Patricia Boyce
ISBN-13: 978-1-960236-08-1

To all who have traveled before me, those who are traveling with me, and those who are starting the journey through the valley of dry bones. Keep following the Light and you will make it through!

Wendy—

It has been such an honor to be a small part of your journey— Keep following the Light—

Patsy

CONTENTS

As We Walk Through the Valley of Dry Bones 1
The Value of Communication 19
The Mind–Body Connection 41
Navigating Depression 61
Living with Grief and What It Can Teach Us 81
Anger Management and Emotional Self-Regulation 99
Our Inner Child and Attachment Style 119
Creating Realistic Expectations 139
The Lazarus Marriage 161
Hope in the Lord 181
About the Author 199
Acknowledgments 201
Notes 205

CHAPTER ONE

As We Walk Through the Valley of Dry Bones

The hand of the LORD was on me, and he brought me out by the Spirit of the LORD and set me in the middle of a valley; it was full of bones.
—***Ezekiel 37:1*** *(NIV)*

Ezekiel was brought out by the Spirit of the Lord and set down in the middle of a valley. If reviewed on a travel website, this valley would not get more than a single star. There was absolutely nothing to recommend it. It was a place without hope, full of dry bones.

I don't know about you, but when I picture this valley, it's not filled with sun-kissed green grass and blooming with flowers that are every color of the rainbow. It's a barren wasteland. The sun is either baking those bones bleach white or is hidden behind clouds, leaving the bone carpet shadowed in gloom. It's definitely not a place we would want to visit.

Would it surprise you to know that many of us not only visit this place but decide to stay? We pitch a tent there and go on to buy the barren land for ourselves, eventually passing it on to our children and grandchildren.

This is what we do when we're struggling with anxiety, anger, or depression. We take ourselves to the valley of dry bones, this desert landscape that's empty of life. It's a place where we go when we can't find connection with others. It's where we go when we blame ourselves for everything wrong that happens to us. When we can't find meaning in our lives and purpose evades us, we turn this desolate land into our home.

We're overwhelmed with emotions and can't or won't make changes. We build our camp around the fear and hide out until the uncomfortable becomes comfortable. Doing something different would only lead to greater discomfort, so we avoid doing what we should do: leave.

We may not even know there's a problem unless someone tells us. Whether we are unaware of the problem or can't bring ourselves to change, we pass it down to our children like an inheritance, and they follow the same unhealthy pattern. In this way, families become mired in the valley of dry bones for generations.

QUESTIONING EVERYTHING AND SEEKING RELIEF

People often refer to dry seasons in their lives and their spiritual walks as time spent in a desert or a valley. We've all been there. I've certainly spent a few seasons wondering, "How much drier can this life get?"

Several years ago, I had an amazing experience with the Lord at what was called a women's silent retreat. This meant no outside interaction for thirty-six hours. It started on a Thursday night with a group praise and worship time. At this retreat, we learned the importance of keeping the boundaries of the silence—no phone calls, texts, news, or Candy Crush. Nothing but preloaded music, the Bible study, and the Lord. We were given a card to show people if we chose to go out of the hotel room to explain that we were not being rude when we didn't talk.

This was thirty-six hours of trusting that family and friends would be okay without me responding to them. It was thirty-six hours of trusting that I would be okay without talking to my husband. I decided to stay in my room the entire time. I was prepared for this and had plenty of food and songs with me as well as multiple Bibles so I could focus on talking to Jesus. It was an amazing experience. Talk about being spiritually overwhelmed! I came home with an entire notebook full of notes.

My husband had prayed for me on this retreat and had asked me to tell him when I returned home what the Lord spoke to me. He likes to joke that he wasn't prepared for pages and pages! I attended the retreat not long after we were called to take the lead at a campus, and I returned with renewed resolve for the direction our lives and the ministry were taking us.

This was a bittersweet opportunity because it came as a result of losing a family we ministered with for years. We loved them and didn't understand the politics of everything. It was sweet because it was an amazing opportunity to continue the work they had started at that campus. My husband and I were both young in the pastoring, so to speak, and knew that God was calling us out of our comfort.

However, the next year, the same retreat didn't bring me the same joy. The expectations I brought along weren't met. I harbored a lot of frustration related to stubborn strongholds we were dealing with in our church ministry, and eventually those frustrations just plain wore down my empathy.

I found myself questioning what seemed like everything: my role, my contributions, my value. I looked around for mentoring, but there was none. I didn't feel received or acknowledged in any area of my life.

Since we first started in the ministry many years before, I held the belief that my role was to support my husband. That was my mission field. But this time felt different. At this retreat, as I went through a Bible study by Lisa Harper, God asked me directly, "Are you willing to labor in obscurity at home, at church, and in your family?"

I didn't have an answer for Him—not then, not yet.

I wrote in my journal that my motivation and energy were low. Like dry bones, I had lost my connection. At the end of the retreat, I decided that my role was still to support my husband and to stay obscure. Inside, however, I yearned for connection. This was a place I hadn't been before. Usually, I walk in my spiritual authority, but this took me back to a previous hurt I'd endured.

I realized that I was acting like a wounded soldier. I saw it and knew what the problem was, but I had a hard time deciding to fix the problem. I came home fragile and disconnected. I journaled. I read. I worshiped. None of it brought me relief. Why? There was no connection. There was no effort on my part or from others to explore what was going on in my mind and body. I set up my camp in the valley of dry bones.

If you're like me, you look around for someone who hears your cries from the valley or desert, someone who will prophesy or be a spiritual mentor. There are very few who step into that role, maybe because they're experiencing dry bones of their own. Perhaps I didn't let people know in a way they could hear, or—let's be honest—maybe they didn't have the care capacity.

If you are in the valley of dry bones today, I want you to know that you're not alone. I found my way out of this valley that no one should visit, let alone live in. This book is your guide through the valley to the new life that Scripture promises. The Holy Spirit is using these words to prophesy to your dry bones.

The dry bones Ezekiel confronted were scattered throughout the valley. When Ezekiel prophesied to the bones as God commanded him to do, "the bones came together, bone to its bone" (Ezekiel 37:7 NASB). Then "tendons were on them, and flesh grew and skin covered them" (Ezekiel 37:8 NASB). The bones were connected. That's the first step God takes in bringing dry bones back to life.

CREATED FOR CONNECTION

I am a licensed professional counselor, and connection is the first thing I look for when meeting with new clients. The questions I ask steer them toward answers that help me to see where they are in their lives. What are they involved in when it comes to family and community activities? What's their social life like? How do they spend their weekends? What hobbies bring them joy? Then I ask them if they belong to a church and if they're connected inside that place of worship.

There are many points of connection in our lives, and it's easy to take them for granted. Some people I meet are new arrivals to our community, and they might not have anticipated the loss of connection they would experience after moving. Suddenly, they're in an unfamiliar place. They don't know anyone. They don't know how things are done.

A common reaction is to withdraw. It's a defense mechanism we use to escape from situations that we find psychologically challenging or emotionally difficult. People use all kinds of activities to withdraw. Some spend hours in front of the television. Others immerse themselves for days in fantastical video-game worlds. Some people sleep more.

While withdrawal is an attempt to protect ourselves from

a real or perceived threat, it may actually result in more pain, stress, and anxiety. This type of withdrawal is counterproductive and self-sabotaging and may even lead to depression.

However, withdrawing for a limited time for the purpose of refocusing on God, rejuvenating the spirit, and aligning needs with boundaries is helpful. Think about when Jesus needed some time away from the crowds to be with the Father and pray. Luke's Gospel account tells us, "The news about him spread all the more, so that crowds of people came to hear him and to be healed of their sicknesses. But Jesus often withdrew to lonely places and prayed" (Luke 5:15–16 NIV). Mark's Gospel recounts that after a few busy days of healing those in distress, "Very early in the morning, while it was still dark, Jesus got up, left the house and went off to a solitary place, where he prayed" (Mark 1:35 NIV).

Withdrawal becomes maladaptive when the root of the pain, stress, and anxiety is not addressed and the period of disconnection lasts far too long. Jonah, for example, withdrew to avoid his mission from God (Jonah 1:1–3). He was avoiding his responsibility and disobeying God.

Withdrawal is disconnection, and the enemy can use it to pull us away from the "living water" (John 4:10–14; 7:37–39) so that we will become spiritually dehydrated. Feeling alone, disconnected from the Source and from others, dries us out in a spiritual sense just as lack of water dries out our bodies. When we speak about connection, it's more than simply hanging out with people. It's about having a purpose.

How Do We Know If We're Experiencing Dry Bones?

There are four characteristics of a person who is experiencing dry bones in his or her life: lack of purpose, lack of meaning, incorrect claiming of blame, and guilt for being "bad" when he or she is not. I look for these characteristics in myself, and it will be helpful for you to watch out for them as well as we help each other to find the way out of the lifeless valley.

Our brains are wired to make meaning of things. God built us that way. We're constantly making meaning. If we're trying to make sense of what our role is and we find ourselves blocked in some way, life may start to feel meaningless.

When this happens in our relationships with other people or in the context of a community, we tell ourselves, "Well, okay, I'm not part of this." When we see others being part of something but don't feel that we are, we lose our sense of purpose. Without purpose, we cannot make meaning. Our perspective may become twisted to the point that we blame ourselves for a perceived failure, even if we're not at fault. We feel guilty for being "bad" when we're not.

I'm not talking about the sinful nature of man. This type of self-blame is another way of trying to make meaning. Children take this approach all the time. Think about it. When something negative happens in childhood, the child's mind may assume that his or her parents couldn't be at fault, because they're good and right, so it has to be the child's fault, even though it isn't.

Similarly, as an adult, you may think, "I've done wrong, and that's why I'm being treated this way or have this loss in my life." Sometimes people make themselves out to be the villains when they're actually the victims of someone else's sinful nature. I don't mean "victim" in a deprecating way. It's a matter of taking too much responsibility for situations that may be beyond your control. When you think that something is your fault, you transition to problem-solving based on that flawed assumption.

OUT OF THE VALLEY

There's a way free of the valley of dry bones. It's a path God has shown us.

Recall that when Ezekiel prophesied as God told him to do, the bones were reconnected; they were put back together into the shape they were supposed to form. However, they still lacked life. They lacked breath (Ezekiel 37:7–8).

God told Ezekiel, "Prophesy to the breath, prophesy, son of man, and say to the breath, 'Thus says the Lord GOD: 'Come from the four winds, O breath, and breathe on these slain, that they may live'" (Ezekiel 37:9 NKJV).

Ezekiel obeyed, and the Lord breathed new life into the dry bones (Ezekiel 37:10). They were reborn, just as we are.

Let's approach this from a practical standpoint. God grants us the breath of life because He knows that dealing with the mind and the soul starts with dealing with the body. That's why we need to breathe.

Breathing is our first line of defense against harmful emotions. That's what I teach for anxiety and anger management. If you breathe from the diaphragm, with a structure and a rhythm in place, you interrupt the panic. You start thinking again.

Imagine a hostage situation, with your emotions as the terrorists. They're holding your rational thinking captive, and breathing is the rescuer that will free you.

So, try this. Put your hands on your stomach, and as you breathe, count to four. Hold for a count of four, release for a count of four, and hold again for a count of four. Continue this for four cycles, or as you visualize rounding the corners of a square.

The reason to put your hands on your stomach while you breathe is to help you stay focused on breathing from the diaphragm. When you breathe in, the stomach will go out. When you breathe out, the stomach will go in. It's like blowing up a balloon and then letting the air out.

My experience is that we tend not to breathe in this manner. Yes, I know. Few, if any, of us like to think about our bellies inflating. Most of us would love for them to stay flat! However, breathing from the upper body, lifting your shoulders and expanding your chest, is stress-related breathing.

Let's face it: we live in a stress-inducing world and are often in a hypervigilant state, especially if we have anxiety. Once the fight-or-flight response is activated, it takes our systems thirty minutes, on average, to return to their normal state. It may be more or less time, depending on the level of the threat or the trigger. Thirty minutes may not sound like a long time, but when fear has you in its grip, seconds can feel like hours.

Intentional breathing exercises help our systems to rest. The thinking side then comes back online, like a biological reboot, enabling us to respond instead of react. The goal is to handle whatever we're facing instead of reacting to it and freezing in fear.

The calm, controlled cycle of breathing in and out for counts of four is useful during those moments of fight-or-flight reactions and bottom-up processing, but it's also a beneficial exercise to practice on a daily basis. We need to learn to use breath to calm and relax our systems when there's no real-life, physical threat, even if our minds are screaming at us that there is one.

You see, our brains can't tell the difference between real-life, physical threats and perceived emotional threats. Most of the time, our brains treat those problems as one and the same thing. Let me put it another way. Your brain will react in the same way whether you're being attacked by a bear or rejected by your peers. Fear is fear, and fear leads us deep into the valley of dry bones.

We see a bit of that in the story of David and Goliath (1 Samuel 17). The Israelites feared the Philistines. They built a camp around that fear and spent all their time talking about it, but they never actually came up with any solutions.

I imagine that they were angry. They probably commiserated over the wrongs being done to them or took it out on themselves and each other. As in most of the other Old Testament accounts, they even questioned God. They settled in for the long haul, waiting in fear for Goliath to strike. Perhaps they held on to a glimmer of hope that the giant warrior would eventually get tired and go home, but that wouldn't have truly eliminated the fear since Goliath could always have come back.

Then David showed up. He was just a kid. And what did that kid have to contribute? David said that there was something wrong. The people of God shouldn't be afraid. They should fix the problem. David was willing to face the fear head-on.

It's rare that adults will listen to a kid, especially one telling them what to do. The army of Israel was camped out in a relatively safe and comfortable place. They had stalled out because change is hard. Sometimes what's needed is the jolt that comes from a message like the one David delivered: "There is hope."

We need to take steps if we're going to walk out of the valley of dry bones. The good news is, well, the Good News! We have an advocate with the Father in Jesus Christ, our Savior, and He has told us many times that we don't have to fear. We can approach life another way.

We can take the helping hand and be led out of the valley of dry bones. We don't have to punish ourselves over and over again with negative, self-deprecating, self-defeating thoughts and behaviors.

Christ Himself endured the pain and horror of crucifixion so that, through His death and resurrection, our relationship with the Father would be restored. He was raised up on the cross, but He wasn't up there forever. His time of trial and tribulation had a limit. The Father took His Son down and brought Him into His loving arms.

Jesus gained that freedom, and so can you. You don't have to keep nailing yourself up there over and over again, grappling with whatever it is that plagues you. Come down off your cross. Let God breathe new life into those dry bones.

WORKBOOK

Chapter One Questions

Question: What are some indications that a person might be in the valley of dry bones? Do you see any of these signs in yourself?

1) Lack of Purpose - No!
2) Lack of Meaning - No.
*3) Incorrect claim of blame - yes
4) Guilt for being "bad." - No!

Yes. Blaming myself for my financial failures + for marrying Eric - He was misleading. I was naive @ mental illness.

Question: David met fear with faith. What fear do you need to face head-on?

Finances + aging alone. I need to continue to prepare the new business, contact an attorney + find out about 14-15 year time frames.

Question: In what area of your life would you like to gain freedom? Into what area would you like God to breathe new life?

Emotional + financial freedom. Understanding + being confident in my mental health + life choice decisions.

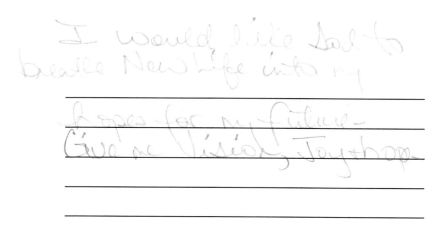

I would like God to breathe New Life into my hopes for my future. Give me Vision, Joy + hope.

Action: Review the breathing technique described in this chapter. Take some time now to practice breathing in this way. How does your body feel as you do this exercise? What do you experience mentally and emotionally?

Chapter One Notes

4x4x4 breathing calms & helps me sleep.

CHAPTER TWO

The Value of Communication

Several years ago, a new client came into my office. To say that she was an animated individual would be an understatement. Imagine a hurricane or a tornado, with winds barreling through a tranquil town and disrupting everything in their path. I thought that maybe I should check behind her to see if she'd knocked over anything on her way in.

She flailed around and flopped on the couch. "I'm crazy," she said.

How do you respond to a statement like that? Well, I had plenty of time to formulate an answer, because she went on and on about how the hospital where she'd spent time in an inpatient unit had decided that she was crazy. I knew that I needed to make a connection with her, to see if we could find a way out of this valley of dry bones into which she'd either wandered or let herself be dragged.

"Okay, so you're crazy. Now what?" I didn't argue with her about whether or not she was, by her definition or anyone else's, crazy. It's my belief that we all have some kind of crazy. It just shows itself in different ways and at different times for different people. Starting the discussion with an acknowledgment of what this woman was saying and where she thought she was helped me to build a rapport with her.

We had to bring the conversation around to what it means to *look* crazy, in her words, as opposed to *being* crazy. I agreed with her that some of her behaviors appeared that way and, as a result, that's how people saw her. They saw her as being loud, erratic, and destructive. They couldn't see past the outward behavior and were either incapable of or unwilling to hear what she was trying to say.

We needed to get to the bottom of the reason why she was doing those things. It turned out that she was acting the way she was acting because she had needs that weren't being met. She wasn't being heard. Instead, she was being devalued. A terrible history of childhood abuse at the hands of her mother came to light. That abuse had been triggered by a recent event. The there and then was impacting the here and now.

So yes, she looked crazy, and she acted crazy. But she wasn't crazy. The only way to dig up that evidence and reveal what was truly going on was to look past the outer person and explore underneath the surface through clear communication. This woman's faith and love of the Lord would not have been revealed if we hadn't been willing to look past outward behavior and appearances.

WHAT DOES CLEAR COMMUNICATION LOOK LIKE?

We often take clear communication for granted. Sure, we have all been taught how to speak. We have conversations with other people every day. We tell the young person behind the drive-up window what burger we want. We ask the grocery-store clerk where to find an item when the shelf contents have been rearranged for the umpteenth time.

However, when it comes to our feelings, we are not taught how to communicate them well, and this leads to problems for us and the people around us. It's extremely difficult for us to put ourselves in the position of vulnerability required for the sharing of what we truly feel and experience beneath the surface. Even as believers, we are not keen on dealing with negative emotions. Many of us were taught in our dysfunctional childhoods to suppress the uncomfortable aspects of our lives. Often we've learned some combination of "don't talk, don't trust, don't feel."[1]

Moving beyond these poor communication methods isn't easy, in part because we make life choices that support our continuing in them. In *Secrets of Your Family Tree*, Dave Carder wrote, "Just as people look for spouses who will allow them to practice the relational styles they learned in their dysfunctional childhoods, so too, do they look for churches built on relationship styles with which they are familiar."[2] In our families, our friendships, and our relationships within the church, we tend to perpetuate ineffective or incomplete communication, especially when it comes to our emotions.

The world has also trained us through personal experience that allowing other people to know our vulnerabilities may result in people using that knowledge against us. It's true that our sinful nature craves advantages we can use over other people in case they become enemies instead of allies, but we should never forget that it's Satan who most wants us to feel shame at our vulnerabilities and dysfunction. He is that "roaring lion" that Peter warned of. He "prowls around ... looking for someone to devour" (1 Peter 5:8 NIV). People may try to use our vulnerabilities against us, but the devil most certainly will, and trying to hide or ignore them won't do anything to strengthen our defenses against his attacks. A well-known adage of Alcoholics Anonymous is that "you are only as sick as your secrets."[3]

Speaking of lions that are up to no good, look no further than the classic Disney movie *The Lion King*[4] for a picture of a dysfunctional family and a great example of how an ill-meaning individual can exploit poor communication and personal vulnerabilities for nefarious purposes.

Scar, King Mufasa's brother, covets the throne. He's hungry for it, as hungry as the enemy is for our souls. Scar plays the role of a victim while conspiring behind the scenes to overthrow the throne. He hides his true purposes behind slick words. Scar arranges for the king's death but manipulates young Simba into thinking that Simba is the reason his father is dead and the land is kingless. Scar's words get into the prince's head so deeply that Simba's hostile self-talk takes over. Simba banishes himself from his family and loved ones. He withdraws and loses connections.

After Scar assumes dominion over the pride lands, they turn into the valley of dry bones. The images of Simba's homeland show that the vegetation has been stripped and the rivers are shriveled. The blues, yellows, and emeralds are reduced to a monochrome gray. There are even piles of actual bones.

Meanwhile, Simba grows up in exile. Although he makes a couple of new friends, he still hides his past and is prone to pushing others away. It's not because they've done anything wrong. He carries around his guilt and refuses to see that he's worthy of being in a friendship. Scar's manipulation causes Simba to embrace lies about himself instead of having a frank conversation about what really happened.

Fixing a Lack of Trust and Building Community

In your fight against the devil, who seeks to manipulate you and take advantage of your vulnerabilities, you can find solace and encouragement in John's reassurance that "He who is in you is greater than he who is in the world" (1 John 4:4 NKJV). The lion will not overcome you in the end. However, the Bible also warns about sharing too much with others.

King David was no stranger to betrayal. He wrote, "Even my close friend in whom I trusted, who ate my bread, has lifted up his heel against me" (Psalm 41:9 NASB). In a society that placed tremendous cultural importance on dining together, that must have been devastating for David. It's likely what influenced him to declare in Psalm 118:8–9, "It is better to take refuge in the LORD than to trust in man. It is better to take refuge in the LORD than to trust in princes" (ESV).

However, David didn't choose to be bitter or resentful. Instead, he offered forgiveness. David understood that we would be betrayed by sinful people in this life, but not by God. His son later advised, "Trust in the LORD with all your heart, and do not lean on your own understanding. In all your ways acknowledge him, and he will make straight your paths" (Proverbs 3:5–6 ESV).

Trusting other people may not come naturally or easily, especially if we come from an unhealthy environment or have been betrayed. The most important step is to trust God. Then learn to trust yourself to be able to handle the situation if you are betrayed. As you start to open up, be mindful and wise regarding what you share with whom.

Communicating Emotions

Claudia Black wrote, "To free yourself from the past you must break the rules of silence and compliance."[5] Talking about past wounds we hold inside and the struggles and emotions we would rather hide from the people around us may not be easy or pleasant, but it's essential to our healing and growth.

During the pandemic, I had the honor of hosting a Bible

study over Zoom. It was a small group of amazing wom our meetings, I emphasized that, especially at the time, needed a community and a place where we could connect in an authentic, vulnerable way.

But that was a problem for me, ironically, as the one leading the group. One of my vulnerabilities is that I feel insignificant. Yes, I know that I have a doctorate and have been a mental-health professional for over twenty years, but in the midst of a dry-bone valley, none of those facts matter emotionally. My tendency to feel insignificant certainly raised its ugly head in this situation. How was I worthy of leading a Bible study? At the time, I didn't feel any more qualified to lead a Bible study than Simba did to take his place as king. There was not even a Scar whispering in my ear—not a physical one, anyway.

My feelings of being unqualified and insignificant became a barrier to communicating my emotions with the other women in the Bible study. I felt vulnerable, and my emotional investment in these women and our relationship meant that the perceived stakes were high. In this type of situation, the emotional intensity overwhelms me, and I find myself losing access to the logical part of my brain, similar to the fight-or-flight response we discussed in the previous chapter. I lose my ability to stay connected to others in the conversation and to communicate my own emotions effectively.

Like many, if not most, other people, I find it easier to power through the work on my own than to share what's going on beneath the surface. In a clinical setting, I don't have to share with my clients, but that wasn't an option when it came to the ladies in that group. It's not as if they wouldn't have noticed if I had tried to hide what I was going through. They were definitely bold enough to call me out, and on a couple of occasions, they did. The bottom line was that I couldn't get away with asking these women to do something I was not willing to do.

Communicating with God

The inability or unwillingness to communicate can raise huge roadblocks to connection. If we don't start by being genuine and authentic, how can we expect other people to be this way with us? We spend our lives posturing toward others and masking our true selves. We "Christianize," for lack of a better word, the version of ourselves that we show other people, not wanting to appear in a negative light.

As Dave Carder pointed out, we tend to be attracted to a church community that is reflective of our family of origin. We bring our attachment style into our relationships within the church. Sometimes we act out our childhood hurts on the pastor or lay leaders.

In many cases, our difficulty in communicating and connecting with other people spills over into our communication with God. Why is that? Scripture teaches us that God loves us and wants us to be restored to fellowship with Him. Well, God is also the Father. He is an authority figure, albeit a holy and loving one. If we haven't had a good relationship—or, possibly, any relationship—with our earthly fathers, we may struggle with knowing how to view and communicate with our heavenly Father.

We may withdraw from genuine connection with God and with other believers and find ourselves merely going through the rituals and routines of church, which leaves us feeling isolated and unfulfilled. We're searching for God but instead wander into the valley of dry bones. We may say, "Well, I read my devotions every morning," or "I'm following a Bible reading plan," but we're not truly connecting with the truth and power of Scripture.

Part of the problem may be that we're communicating with God in a defensive manner. We put up barriers or don our masks, trying to Christianize ourselves before the Creator of the universe, who already knows our inmost thoughts and feelings, our very hearts and souls. People have come to me and said, "I can't question God." My response is: "Why not? Why do you feel that you aren't allowed to question God? What does the Bible say about it?"

The Bible is full of people questioning God. The book of Habakkuk is all about asking the Lord, "Why are You doing what You are doing?" Job, in his great suffering, asked God questions throughout the book that bears his name. David begged for answers in the Psalms. Look at the stories of the sisters Mary and Martha. Martha was so bold as to go to Jesus and question Him, not once but twice (Luke 10:38–42; John 11:17–27).

Should we be shocked at these accounts? No! What we're actually seeing is healthy communication. People asked the Lord, "Why?" and He responded to them, just like He will respond to us. We need to put ourselves in a position to communicate openly and honestly with God. He should be the first one we go to when we need to sort through how we're feeling and the reason we're experiencing those emotions. Sharing our inner selves with God will help us to find the words and the confidence to express our emotions in a healthy way. We also need to remember that talking with God is meant to be a two-way conversation. We should be listening to God as well as speaking. We may not always hear what we want to hear, but we need to listen anyway.

STAY IN YOUR LANE

If you want to show people instantly that you don't value what they're saying, cut them off mid-sentence, either by jumping into the conversation, bringing up a new topic, or turning the focus back to yourself. How many times have you experienced this kind of unbalanced conversation? Isn't it annoying?

This happens often in communication between spouses, friends, and relatives. It's especially common for individuals who experience ADD or ADHD. These interruptions make having a conversation extremely difficult. I find trying to jump back into the exchange exhausting because I have to figure out where and when to begin. I end up thinking, "Why should I bother?" and am left with the impression that what I'm trying to say isn't worth expressing.

Years ago, I worked with a woman—let's call her Lois—who constantly cut me off when we were in a group setting.

I wanted to practice being assertive, and a relationship with lower emotional risks seemed like a good place to start. Years prior to this, I was told that it wasn't that I said something; it was how I said it. I wanted to start doing something different. After praying and practicing breathing, I knocked on Lois's office door and asked her if I could talk with her. I focused intentionally on what she did and said versus who she was, the behavior instead of the person. It's difficult for us to separate people, ourselves and others, from their behaviors. Generally, we believe that the person, not the behavior itself, is the problem.

I said to Lois, "It seems like when we are in a group setting, I tend to get interrupted. I wondered if you have any awareness of this happening." It was time to be forthright.

Lois went on the defensive, of course, but I immediately noted, "It looks like there is some defensiveness here. Is there?"

"Nope," she said. I wasn't sure if my being assertive would improve the situation, but she did add, "I'll make sure I don't interrupt you again."

"Thank you. I really appreciate working with you." Notice that I didn't directly accuse Lois, and I attempted to approach her in a healthy manner. I didn't want to call out her behavior in front of everyone, but I also didn't believe that I needed to accept it. I was practicing assertiveness, which meant that I was seeking to express my needs while respecting both myself and Lois. This was my attempt at setting healthy boundaries within the relationship.

I went back to my office and didn't share this conversation

with anyone else. My communication efforts didn't result in an immediate fix. Lois spent several weeks in cold anger, also known as the silent treatment, avoiding any conversation with me. She would intentionally walk away when I approached the group, but she no longer interrupted me. I waited it out, and eventually she came around.

I later learned that Lois had ADHD/ADD. This became an example to remind me to recognize that someone's motives may not be to hurt intentionally. It may be a case of limited awareness on both sides. Healthy communication brought awareness and helped us to navigate our relationship with greater understanding.

Interruptions and distractions can be deadly to relationships. In the case of me and Lois, we were able to restore communication and continue working together. In other situations, recovery may not be possible or necessary as God grows us in different ways.

There was a time when I would hang out with a couple of friends. We would go to breakfast or dinner together, maybe get coffee or ice cream when the mood struck. It sounds great on the surface, doesn't it? The problem for me was that it seemed as long as the conversation was geared toward those friends, they could chat away, but whenever I would try to share about my life, they'd become easily distracted. Out would come their phones and their calendars. Often they'd interject stories about people they knew or situations they'd been in, essentially hijacking the topic in a veiled attempt to relate. Invariably, they'd end up redirecting the conversation back to themselves. I would often feel like the third or fourth wheel, depending on how many of us were together. Whether intentionally or not, these friends were erecting barriers to healthy communication.

I'm not a competitive person, so it was easy to be steamrolled. It was exhausting work to redirect the conversation, and I would end up feeling that what I was trying to say wasn't worth the effort. I had difficulty attempting to use the assertive communication techniques that had helped me before. Instead, I found myself sitting there and nodding, not really being an active participant in the conversation. It was interesting to watch someone else in our group doing the same. Honestly, it felt validating as I would often question if it was just me.

The more I tried to engage, the worse I felt about myself. Would it sound selfish or childish to speak up and voice my concerns and needs? Would I be dismissed or devalued? Maybe I was misreading the situation. I didn't want to jeopardize these friendships. In this situation with high emotional risks, my fear took over and prevented me from practicing the respectful assertiveness I had been able to exercise effectively with Lois.

As a group, we started spending less and less time together, but I continued to reach out with texts and phone calls to keep the connections. It became clear that I was the initiator in the relationships and this season in our lives had faded away. The loss was sad at the time, but it was healthy for me in the long run. I still love those friends and am confident that we could pick up where we left off, but I realized that the enemy was using my vulnerability against me in that context.

God's direction took the difficult decision to set boundaries out of my hands. He needed to grow us in different ways.

THE JOY AND POWER OF EFFECTIVE COMMUNICATION

The Bible offers us lessons from the master communicator, Jesus. He was clear and forthright, whether He was imparting a direct instruction to His disciples or weaving a moral into one of His many parables. Jesus told the disciples plainly, "Therefore consider carefully how you listen. Whoever has will be given more; whoever does not have, even what they think they have will be taken from them" (Luke 8:18 NIV).

Effective communication involves work. It's not just sitting back and letting someone talk while you soak in what he or she is saying and try to prevent your mind from wandering. You must focus your full attention on what the other person is saying. It may require you to ask questions and dig deep to find out what the person is truly thinking and feeling.

We learn in Proverbs 18 that Scripture regards those who don't listen as fools (Proverbs 18:2, 13). It's a small wonder, then, that Jesus listened to others so He could discern their full range of emotions before giving empathic responses designed to invite people into deeper conversation with Him. He demonstrated a desire to learn more about people, and He listened in a nonjudgmental way. Jesus didn't listen with the purpose of finding some character flaw or behavior to criticize but so He could explore areas that needed change.

When we're listening to someone, the goal of our responses should be to clarify what we've heard the other person express. My therapist friends call me the "help-me-to-understand lady." Questions such as "Would you help me to understand?" and "Would you help me to understand what you understood me to say?" offer the person with whom you are speaking the opportunity to clarify what he or she meant as well as specify how he or she interpreted your words. That way, you have a greater chance of understanding each other. Now my therapist friends are using this type of question, too.

DR. NAY'S ROADBLOCKS TO EFFECTIVE COMMUNICATION

In his book *Taking Charge of Anger*, Dr. W. Robert Nay offers a helpful list of "roadblocks to effective communication."[6] Though he focuses on a specific emotion, his advice on things not to say is relevant to any conversation, especially one involving conflict. Here are common communication roadblocks Dr. Nay says to avoid putting up:

"You-tooing." For example, "I may have interrupted you, but you interrupt me all the time" doesn't move the conversation forward.

Past "historicizing." This involves drawing on past situations, events, and interactions and may begin with phrasing like: "What about last year when you...?"

Overgeneralizations. These include blanket statements such as: "You always forget something."

Labeling. For instance, "You are irrational" characterizes someone in a generalized, unhelpful way.

Mind reading. Making assumptions, like "I know you are angry with me," doesn't tend to placate the other person or defuse conflict the way you might think it would.

Exasperating. Resist the urge to vent frustration with statements such as: "It's just hopeless and exhausting trying to talk with you."

Conversational habits like these are pitfalls that put other people on the defensive in ways that are not conducive to good communication.

LISTENING WITH OUR HEARTS

I like to say that the most effective way to listen is to listen with your third ear: your heart. When I think of listening with the *heart*, I see "hear" in that word, and I think of the "t" at the end as representing the cross. If we listen to others the way Jesus did, we can respond to them like He did and show His love to them. We often talk about seeing others through the eyes of Christ, but what about listening through the ears of the Lord?

James wrote that, as believers, we "should be quick to listen, slow to speak" (James 1:19 NIV). I like to remind people that we have two ears and one mouth for a reason.

Listening well requires staying in the present. Don't let yourself be distracted by past wrongs. Don't let your mind wander off into imaginings of what you have to do tomorrow. Focus on what the other person is saying in that moment.

Listening also requires what is called "holding space" for the other person. People have said to me, "All you do is listen to people all day long. I could do that." Apparently, I make it look easy, and people think, "Well, if she can do it, I can, too," because three people in my immediate family are in various stages of a professional counseling career.

Of course, it's not truly that simple. Intentional listening is hard work. My brain and muscles are sore at the end of a good, long day. As a counselor, my goal isn't to be heard, but to minister to the other person.

There's a great scene in the movie *Hope Springs* that relates to the goal of serving others. This scene conveys what we're trying to accomplish when we seek to improve our communication and resurrect a relationship that has become stuck in the valley of dry bones. Tommy Lee Jones and Meryl Streep play a married couple who attend a weeklong counseling intensive in an effort to renew their thirty-year marriage. Steve Carell, as the marriage counselor, asks them a vital question:

"Ultimately, I think you have to ask yourself, 'Is this person worth more to me than my pride?'"[7]

That's what we need to ask ourselves every time we enter a conversation: "Is this person worth more than my pride? Can I value what this person is trying to say more than what I want to say, at least for this short span of time together?" If our answer is "yes," we are ready to take crucial steps out of the valley of dry bones and toward a land in which healthy, direct communication is the bedrock of solid, affirming relationships with our colleagues, friends, and loved ones.

WORKBOOK

Chapter Two Questions

Question: What barriers do you have to communicating your emotions to God? What scriptures support the idea that you should be open with God about what you are thinking and feeling?

1) I'm embarrassed by my current marriage + financial circumstances. However, what if this is God's plan?

All of Psalms — Confirms I can be open w/ God.

Question: What barriers do you have to communicating your emotions to other people? What risks do you need to take in order to share your emotions with your family members, friends, and colleagues?

Same — I'm embarrassed. I don't want to be judged.

Choose wisely whom to confide in.

Question: What boundaries do you need to set in order to have healthier relationships that allow and help you to grow in the direction God is leading you?

Wisdom + self control to share w/ the appropriate people.

Action: Review Dr. Nay's list of communication roadblocks and determine which one(s) you tend to use in different contexts and with different people. Come up with a plan to avoid these pitfalls and begin developing healthy communication habits. *mind reading*

Chapter Two Notes

CHAPTER THREE

The Mind–Body Connection

We can't talk about the mind without involving the body, and vice versa. This concept is nothing new. Plato's dialogue *Charmides* includes the adage, "As you ought not to attempt to cure the eyes without the head, or the head without the body, so neither ought you to attempt to cure the body without the soul ... for the part can never be well unless the whole is well."[8]

And centuries later, Christ ministered to the body well before He addressed what was at the root of people's problems. They came to Him with all kinds of ailments, and His first response was to heal, not lecture. He didn't make them wait around in pain while He dug to the heart of the spiritual or psychological issue that was at play.

Take the crippled man who waited for help by the pool near the Sheep Gate. The Aramaic word for this pool was *Bethesda* (John 5:2), which means "house of mercy."[9] This is fitting given the healing that supposedly took place there.

There were many invalids—"the blind, the lame, the paralyzed" (John 5:3 NIV)—gathered there in hopes of a miracle.

When Jesus was passing by the pool on His way to a Jewish feast being held in Jerusalem, He saw a man lying there "who had been an invalid for thirty-eight years" (John 5:1, 5 ESV). What was His first question to that man? It wasn't to address sin in his life or to ask about his mental well-being.

"Do you want to be healed?" Jesus asked (John 5:6 ESV). Of course, the man did, but he hadn't taken action to get the help he needed. He replied, "Sir, I have no one to put me into the pool when the water is stirred up, and while I am going another steps down before me" (John 5:7 ESV).

This man's condition wasn't only physical. His victim mentality held him back psychologically as well. He was unwilling to take the steps, mentally speaking, to get past his predicament. Do you see how he placed the blame on others? He might have been thinking, "I've been sitting on this mat for more than thirty years because people are rude and inconsiderate."

We're no strangers to this kind of mentality today. When it comes to emotions like anxiety and anger, for example, we still allow our physical state to determine who we are. We say, "It's not my fault, you know, when I get angry," or "There was nothing I could do, because I was anxious." And, of course, there's the classic: "I just ate that entire chocolate cake because I was anxious. The stress made me do it."

The last example is a bit facetious, but I think you understand the point. Emotional eating struggles are real.

THE BODY AND LITERAL DRY BONES

It all starts with fear. There is so much to know about how anxiety and stress affect us, but I want to focus on one specific point. When we are stressed, our bodies release a stress hormone called cortisol, which wreaks havoc on our systems. High levels of cortisol suppress our immune systems, leaving us more vulnerable to infection and disease, increased weight gain, concentration problems, and other negative impacts on our health.

Our bodies recognize this danger and, to help bring themselves back into balance, counter the cortisol by taking calcium from our bones and teeth. It's an attempt to neutralize the cortisol, like how antacid neutralizes stomach acid when indigestion comes calling. The calcium is doing its best to reset our bodies to neutral.

The problem is that when this stress or anxiety becomes chronic, our bodies are constantly releasing cortisol and then trying to make up for that by using the calcium we have stored up. You can see where this is going, I hope. There isn't a way for our diets to replenish the drained calcium fast enough to stave off the constant buildup of cortisol. As a result, our bones are leached of the calcium they need to stay strong. They can potentially become weaker and more brittle, a sure sign of osteoporosis. We develop, in effect, literal dry bones. Arthritis?

Now, you might argue with the assertion that we can't maintain this balance through diet. Surely, you say, the simple answer is to eat more dairy! My husband would agree with you 100 percent.

Contrary to what my husband fervently believes, the answer is to breathe, not to eat more ice cream. This is where the breathing techniques I mentioned previously come into play—though I won't begrudge anyone a pint of ice cream now and then!

FINDING CLARITY THROUGH CONSCIOUS BREATHING

When we're anxious about something, we tend either to hold our breath or to breathe in a shallow, rapid manner. Breathing this way makes us inhale more oxygen than we exhale carbon dioxide. The effects can be felt immediately. This short breathing restricts the blood supply to the brain, and that, in turn, may cause dizziness. We may experience numbness or tingling in our hands and feet. Some people even lose consciousness.

This link to breathing is evident in the way anxiety can also trigger or worsen symptoms of asthma. I once had a client whom I'll call Alana. She was referred to me by her insurance company. They were concerned because Alana had taken many trips to the emergency room because of her asthma. Was it possible that she was experiencing more of a psychological issue than a physical one?

Alana agreed to work with me. She was reluctant, but the insurance company had told her that they wouldn't continue paying for her ER visits if she didn't undergo therapy. I say "reluctant" because she believed that her problems were completely physical. "There's nothing wrong with me otherwise," she insisted.

Alana's reluctance continued through the intake process, which I would say she tolerated rather than embraced. What was interesting was that she admitted during my questioning that her husband exhibited negative behaviors, and she took the opportunity to announce, "But I don't ever plan to leave him." I hadn't even posed that as a question.

Long story short, we eventually made connections between her husband's behaviors and her asthma attacks, which were triggered by her anxiety about his behaviors. This realization helped Alana to take a hard look at how her anxiety was affecting her asthma.

As we worked together, her asthma improved, and she learned healthier coping skills to manage her anxiety. She learned to lean into Scripture, identify primary emotion triggers, incorporate deep breathing, process thoughts through journaling, practice assertive communication, develop healthy boundaries, and apply self-care techniques. She also learned how to recognize enabling behaviors and body awareness.

Over the same period of time, her husband's negative behaviors became worse. This was expected as he pushed back on her newly developed boundaries and ways of relating. It proved to be too much for them to sustain as a couple, and Alana made the painful decision not to continue with the relationship.

Through utilizing the breathing techniques and trusting

the Lord as she practiced healthier coping skills, coupled with the end of a marriage to a difficult person who would not relent in his negative behaviors, Alana found herself no longer wrestling with chronic asthma attacks. Her visits to the ER ended. She was happier, and I can assume that her insurance company was, too.

IT'S A PAIN

Breathing is key when it comes to managing stress and its attendant emotions, and we've seen how anxiety impacts the basic in-and-out reflex that we human beings need to survive. Converting oxygen into carbon dioxide isn't optional.

But anxiety does far more than mess with our breathing. It can inflict damage on our immune system, raise our blood pressure, and lead to coronary problems. It can also upset our gastrointestinal system, leading to issues such as stomach pains, irritable bowel syndrome, and bloating.

Do you remember the fight-or-flight response I mentioned before, the feeling of panic brought on by elevated anxiety or stress? Well, it affects more than your body's vital systems. There's a real danger of strain on the very bits and pieces that get you physically ready to flee.

Muscles are doing all the work in your body. They get you up and keep you moving. They keep you breathing, as we already noted, even when you're not thinking about it. But what about the voluntary muscles? These are the ones that help you to lift your groceries and put one foot in front of the other. When they get ready to run but you don't actually run,

The Mind–Body Connection

it may lead to muscle pain and inflammation. *the enemy of aging well*

When we're gripped by fear, those muscles get themselves into a constant state of contraction. They're ready to go when you need them to, and if you were in an actual emergency, they would be the greatest asset you could hope for. They'd help you to flee from real danger.

But since we're talking about a situation in which there's perceived danger, not a physical threat, this constant contraction harms your health. Muscle pain and inflammation are among the troublesome issues that arise. The strain may also lead to chronic joint pain, arthritis, fibromyalgia, and chronic exhaustion.

This is something I see on a regular basis in my practice. I have clients tell me that they feel tired after an anxiety or anger event. Anxiety and anger are both physical responses to danger, real or perceived. Have you experienced that feeling of exhaustion? It's no wonder! The body has been holding those muscles as if you were running a marathon. When you can finally relax a bit, the muscles are exhausted.

Let's put it another way. Think about holding something heavy for a long time. You can feel the burn, so to speak, in whatever muscles you're using to support the weight. Once you drop the weight, the muscles that have been doing all the work need a chance to rest and recover. They're worn out, at least temporarily.

With anxiety, however, we don't give ourselves that recovery time. We don't grant ourselves the grace to take a step back and realize, "Something is wrong here." We may be triggered into yet another anxiety event before there's a chance to recover from the last one.

Weight gain is another negative result of anxiety. A lot of factors come together to impact digestion, and slowed digestion can lead to weight gain as well as fatigue. Fatigue then saps our motivation to exercise. We simply don't want to get up and do the thing we logically know will help us to be healthier and feel better. Some of us seek out comfort foods that are sugary or carbohydrate-heavy in an effort to cope with anxiety. Think about how many people have commented, either publicly or in your private life, about how much weight they put on during the height of the COVID-19 pandemic. I've even told others that I put on a few "COVID pounds."

STRESS IS NORMAL; CHRONIC STRESS ISN'T

That said, I don't intend to pass judgment on stress as being something bad. Stress serves a purpose, as does the fight-or-flight response. There may be times in our lives when we need to fight, and there may be times when we need to flee. The problems occur when our brains apply that stress response to the wrong situations, in which the danger is not real but perceived. It's a mind problem that leads to unhealthy body issues.

So, what is "normal" stress? It actually involves doing things that, in and of themselves, might not be considered normal, as in typical or everyday. Examples may include flying on a plane, going on a first date, taking a big test, or talking in front of a crowd. We experience these things, but perhaps not as often as eating a meal, going to the grocery store, or taking the dog for a walk. When we experience something uncommon or unfamiliar, our minds react to what they interpret as a dangerous situation. This reaction manifests as anything from gentle uneasiness to terrible distress, from being confused or concerned to being downright afraid.

The anxiety we experience preceding and during uncommon events is healthy when it helps us to stay alert and aware in the face of something new or rare, but we tend to push through that anxiety and do whatever it is anyway. We board the plane even though we're nervous. We go on the first date while suppressing the butterflies in our stomachs. We power through the test even while our palms are sweating. We make that speech in front of the crowd even though we'd rather sit down in the back row.

Stress becomes unhealthy, however, when we experience obsessive worry or intrusive thoughts and have difficulty making decisions. If we feel panic over everyday events, we are experiencing unhealthy anxiety. It will keep us stuck in what-if fantasies and "should I" doubts. It becomes about us, not about the event.

We may magnify our anxiety by blowing things out of proportion, minimize concerns through reducing them to unimportance, or personalize them by taking on too much blame for the negatives that might happen—putting ourselves up on that cross, so to speak. We try to rehearse, read minds, or forecast in an effort to be prepared. Most often, our predictions are unlikely. We end up avoiding anxiety-inducing situations because of those distorted fears and then inating over them even more, which may lead to depression.

We believe that avoiding triggering events will help us, but this coping technique ultimately feeds the anxiety. We tell ourselves that we need to avoid certain situations in order to feel better. We believe that the only way to stay calm is not to do the certain thing or to do it with obsessive-compulsive behaviors.

The cognitive distortions of what-ifs, "should" statements, rehearsing, mind reading, and forecasting are all unhealthy coping skills as they send messages that we have to be completely prepared for everything. This is irrational and only reinforces that if we don't do these things, we won't be calm. The constant obsession with avoiding stressful situations affects our bodies and our actions until we take our tents and make camp in the very place we want to avoid.

I Think I Am

If you're experiencing unhealthy stress and anxiety, you may wonder, "Why is this happening to me? How do I quit having these thoughts that lead to such negative effects?"

It's not only about *what* we think, but also *how* we think. We tend to believe that what we feel is based on external factors, something or someone else. This has been a human tendency since Adam and Eve in the garden of Eden (Genesis 3:12–13). In short, we blame others for how we feel: "He made me so angry," or "She made me so upset."

This puts us squarely into the victim role and implies that

we have no control over our feelings. We believe that it's not our fault when we feel anxious or angry, and we look outside of ourselves to find someone or something to make us feel better.

The truth is that external events don't make us feel a certain way. Rather, *our interpretation* of external events produces our feelings. We can be invited, influenced, impacted, or triggered in our emotions, but when it comes down to it, we make the final call about how we interpret what we've experienced and how we react. Our beliefs and attitudes about what's happening shape our feelings and motivate us to react in the ways we do.

Unrealistic, irrational, self-defeating, and self-sabotaging thoughts direct our feelings toward negative outcomes. We may not plan it this way, but our thoughts are often negative. Dr. Daniel Amen, a psychiatrist and brain disorder specialist, calls them Automatic Negative Thoughts, or ANTs.[10] These thoughts push our feelings about a person, a thing, or an event in a negative direction, which then affects our behavior.

ANTS are like reflexes that impact our behaviors, emotions, bodies, and decisions without our realizing it. They stem from our beliefs about ourselves and the world, which flow like a river in the background of our minds and sometimes pop into our conscious thinking.

If thoughts lead to emotions and behaviors, it stands to reason that changing the way we think changes the way we feel, which, in turn, changes the way we behave. We can train our brains to improve our responses. Bingo!

How do we accomplish this? I invite you to challenge your

thoughts. Cognitive distortions have power because we assume them to be facts. Try to find evidence to support a particular thought. If a thought is not based on historical or current fact, then consider it distorted. Challenging and reframing ANTs will cause them to be less automatic and controlling.

Imagine getting pulled over by the police for driving over the speed limit. If you believe that you should never be stopped by the police, then before the officer even pulls you over, your brain will trigger the fight-or-flight process. Your body will tense up. Perhaps you will engage in negative inner talk, such as "Who does he think he is?"

When you begin interacting with the officer, you might exhibit aggressive behavior. You might say something rude or condescending, such as "Where are the donuts?" or "My taxes pay your salary!"

Meanwhile, the negative personal consequences, including neurological, biological, and physiological processes, are stacking up. These processes are the fight-or-flight reaction to a perceived threat. Remember that your brain has a hard time differentiating between an emotional threat and a physical threat. In the case of getting pulled over by the police, the emotional threat is a result of your interpretation of the events through distorted thoughts. If you continue with behaviors based on these distorted thoughts, you may wind up in jail, pulling gravel out of your face, and find yourself trying to convince a judge that you shouldn't have been pulled over in the first place!

Now let's revisit this same hypothetical event, except this

time you hold the belief that you always get stopped. You go into a victim mentality and a self-defeating thought process. You pull over right away. Maybe you overcompensate, even cry, because surely that's never been done before! You won't get handcuffed and taken to jail, but you will drive away in a prison of your own making, repeating, "Oh, I always get stopped." This reaction can lead to depression.

Although the event itself didn't change, your reactions did, based on your underlying beliefs and initial thoughts. Disputing the belief from the get-go means finding the evidence and citing the source to your belief system. Question your assumptions. Where is it written that you should never get stopped? Nowhere. Are there times when you get away with speeding? Yes, but should you? No, because you're not immune to the consequences of breaking the law.

On the other hand, you can also challenge the "I get stopped all the time" assumption. If that were true, a patrol car would be sitting in your driveway every morning. Do you like getting pulled over? No? Well, then, maybe you should stop speeding.

Some people might say that you should lower your expectations, but that's not the right attitude. Instead, you should adjust your expectations to yourself and the world in which you live. Say I have the belief that when I go to a store and a man goes through the door in front of me, he needs to hold it open for me. If this doesn't happen, I might stand and wait—impatiently—or I might blow up at him right off the bat. I could self-deprecate or engage in any number of other unhealthy responses.

The best response would be to adjust my expectations and consider that this man probably doesn't know my personal rules for life. Why should he? I don't go around handing out my rule book to strangers. Maybe he doesn't share the same rules, or maybe he's dealing with his own issues at the moment. I don't have to personalize it. The event doesn't have to ruin my day. My locus of control is internal, not external.

In the context of emotions, *locus of control* is the degree to which we believe that we control actions and consequences. For example, athletes with an external locus of control may blame losing the game on poor coaching, unfair referees, or even other teammates. On the other hand, if they have an internal locus of control, athletes may reflect on their own performance and recognize areas to improve.

Our thoughts, our feelings, and our physical reactions to our emotions are all wrapped up together in a web of connections. What we think and feel has a tremendous impact on our bodies, right down to our very bones. We don't have to be like a horse or mule with a bit in its mouth, as Psalm 32:9 says, having no understanding about why we do what we do. We don't have to be "like a wave of the sea, blown and tossed by the wind," as James described a person with doubts about his or her faith (James 1:6 NIV). We don't have to allow our thoughts and emotions to steer us into the valley of dry bones, as if we don't have any control over them.

The brain is an adaptive organ that gets stronger with exercise. It has the ability to reorganize itself in both structure and function, a characteristic called *neuroplasticity*. The good news is that the brain is constantly learning and rerouting neural pathways. The bad news is that the brain is neutral and doesn't know the difference between good and bad learning. It will learn and store whatever is repeated in thoughts, actions, and behaviors. This is how habits form. What we think becomes what we do.

People who want to break the habit of smoking use another habit to distract themselves until they break free, and then they can dial back those new activities. Similarly, to break the habit of negative thinking, we need to interject a new way of thinking. I like to tell people, "Think about your thinking until you don't have to think about it anymore."

We can train our brains to internalize our locus of control instead of externalizing it. We can identify and challenge our ANTs to lessen their control over us. If we're going to get up from our mats, like the man by the pool of Bethesda, we have to be willing to change how we think.

In the next few chapters, we'll explore what the start of healing might look like for those of us who face certain kinds of challenges in our valley of dry bones, beginning with depression.

WORKBOOK

Chapter Three Questions

Question: In what ways might physical ailments sometimes be caused or exacerbated by emotions?

_____
_____
_____
_____
_____
_____
_____
_____
_____
_____
_____

Question: In what situations do you experience stress? Are these unusual events or everyday occurrences?

_____
_____
_____
_____
_____
_____
_____
_____
_____
_____
_____

Question: What coping methods do you tend to employ to try to avoid or respond to stressful situations?

_____
_____
_____
_____
_____
_____
_____

_____

_____

_____

_____

Action: Consider a recent situation in which you felt anxious or angry and spoke or acted from this emotion. Try to identify one or more underlying thoughts that led to your anxiety or anger. If you have trouble doing this, wait until the next time you experience this feeling and look for a pattern in the thoughts that seem to drive or feed your negative emotion. Then challenge these thoughts. Is there evidence to support them? If not, begin replacing them with truth and continue doing so until they no longer influence your feelings and behavior.

The self sabotage cycle: When you have no real sense of "self" or personhood, you may struggle to make "life choices" that fit, eg, marriage choices, career choices & if those choices are not sustainable - you may feel trapped (financially, emotionally).

Chapter Three Notes

P.47 — I wonder how I will "feel" when this ordeal w/ Marc comes to resolution. I anticipate significant "relief."

→ e.g., When I/we left I ran (2) PR's 10K + 1/2 marathon. I felt like a piano had been lifted off my back.

→ These past 12-24 months have been a gift in my recovery.

→ P.48 Exercise is non-negotiable. I know I must!

→ P.50 "Feeling/believing that I should be prepared for everything" has been a learned thought process. — Clarify? A struggle for "control?"

P.51 It's not happening "to me" but "for me." What if this is God's plan?

CHAPTER FOUR

Navigating Depression

We often have a simplistic view of what depression is. We might picture people who are depressed as spending most of the day in bed, with the covers pulled up, and crying all the time. They might even be suicidal.

I don't intend to minimize the severity of symptoms associated with depression, but the truth is that there are many individuals experiencing depression who don't show anything like those signs. There are times when I mention to clients, "It sounds like there are some signs of depression here," and they respond, "Well, I'm not depressed." It's much like when we talk about alcohol abuse with someone who may be an alcoholic and the response is: "I can't be an alcoholic. I'm not a bum on the sidewalk."

A client reached out to me not long ago, saying, "I've got to have an appointment." I wasn't sure what precisely she needed, but she went on to tell me that her cousin, a man who was always the life of the party, was away on a weekend trip and had called his girlfriend to tell her, "You have to get here right now. I'm contemplating suicide."

The client couldn't wrap her head around that. "How did I miss the signs?" she wondered. "Where did I go wrong?"

Setting aside that my client was assuming herself to be responsible for her cousin's life, she recognized that to everyone around him, he seemed like a fun, outgoing guy. He was experiencing severe depression but appeared to the outside world to be high-functioning.

Depression is a term that's used loosely. It may mean a temporary feeling of sadness, melancholy, and apathy, or it may refer to a diagnosable medical condition, as in the case of clinical depression. It may result from chemical or hormonal imbalances, or it may be situational sadness due to life changes, loss, or other crises.

Sadness is a normal emotion that we feel during challenging times or when facing various life stressors. When that sadness becomes intense and is accompanied by feelings of hopelessness, helplessness, and worthlessness, it can trigger depression, which is not exclusively an emotional issue or a medical issue.

Being depressed is also not a static state. Feelings can change, and moods can worsen. How many times have you heard the phrase "a downward spiral"? It applies to depression as well.

A downward spiral occurs when we feel ourselves slipping into a lower mood. It usually begins with distorted thoughts, including negative beliefs about ourselves and the world. The spiral strengthens those negative beliefs, leading to increased negative feelings and, eventually, depression.

It's a fair maxim to say that the more we do something, the better we get at it. This even applies to negative thoughts. When we focus on the negative in our lives, we see more of it and get better and better at thinking negatively. Those thoughts pile up, and we sink into a defeated, irrational, self-destructive, self-sabotaging spiral that takes us further down into depression.

Think of it as coming to the edge of the valley of dry bones. You see what it looks like as you approach it: a desolate wasteland. You know that the deeper you go into it, the more lost you'll be, but you get turned around because everything there looks the same. You may pass the same pile of bones many times without even noticing. That doesn't help your mind to make sense of what direction you're heading, and you become overwhelmed. To alter the familiar phrase somewhat, you can't see the valley for the bones.

We can't always avoid the downward spiral into depression—especially if we're looking only at the big picture of our situation, like that sprawling valley filled with endless heaps of dry bones. We need someone standing outside of the valley, crying out to us like Ezekiel cried into the valley or like John called from the wilderness, guiding us up and out of that downward spiral.

often signs that, when taken together, can help us to make that determination.

First and most importantly, you should immediately seek assistance from qualified health-care professionals if you experience any thoughts of self-harm. My client's cousin I mentioned above took the essential step of calling for help as soon as these dangerous thoughts emerged.

Other signs, while not as immediately life-threatening, can be just as serious:

- Having feelings of emptiness or sadness that last for more than a couple of weeks or are more than normal reactions to a life change
- Lacking interest in activities that once felt purposeful
- Sleeping too much or too little
- Gaining or losing weight without trying
- Having low energy or lack of drive
- Isolating from friends
- Becoming more irritable
- Having an increased sense of guilt or feelings of low self-worth
- Ruminating over mistakes or failures
- Blaming oneself for situations beyond one's control
- Having trouble concentrating

Outward physical signs are helpful to note if you suspect that someone is experiencing depression. Check in with this person about his or her eating and sleeping habits. Changes in social routine, as mentioned above, are vital indicators as well. Also pay attention to how the person acts in front of you. Maybe he or she is moving more slowly or has developed poor eye contact. Maybe this person has become guarded or distant when answering questions. Speech may turn slow and low or, on the other hand, rapid and loud. Poor hygiene, posture, and the inability to control tears are other behaviors that show someone may be dealing with agitating or anxious thoughts.

SEEMINGLY HAPPY

The outward signs of depression are not always obvious. For instance, depressed people might put on a mask of happiness to everyone around them. They may deny the reality of what's going on inside them, even to themselves.

The term *smiling depression* is not a medical diagnosis—or necessarily a clinical term, either—but it's useful to help us describe what happens when people try to manage their depression by hiding their symptoms. These individuals are actively denying that there's a problem: "I'm fine, just fine. Everything is fine."

One of the primary reasons they continue to engage with others instead of withdrawing is because they're fearful of people finding out that there's something wrong with them. It's a bit like *imposter syndrome*, a term that describes when people who could be celebrating their achievements instead doubt their abilities and believe that they don't deserve success, in part because they don't know how to process it.

People who try to conceal their depression may fear losing relationships. Even if they sense that they need help, they may have no idea how to get it, or they may not want to burden others. They can't bring themselves to let other people in, so they justify or rationalize isolating themselves and disconnecting from their community. Because they hide the depression well, other people don't see what's really going on.

It's sad to say, but I frequently find this to be true within the community of believers. The culture of Christianity has historically been judgmental of mental health. We may have multiple medical problems, be actively engaged in sinful behaviors, or struggle in various others areas while still receiving support from our Christian community, but this is often not the case with matters of mental health. This mindset is beginning to shift, and it will continue to shift if believers are willing to get real about their struggles. Finding a place to practice being vulnerable will result in authentic and genuine connections among believers.

People who exhibit smiling depression may use Christianized statements and come across as almost too happy. They make superficial connections, attempting to put the focus on others in an effort to feel better about themselves or to divert attention from themselves so no one has a chance to see their inner struggles. This is a misinterpretation of Philippians 2:3–4, in which Paul advised, "Do nothing out of selfish ambition or vain conceit. Rather, in humility value others above yourselves, not looking to your own interests but each of you to the interests of the others" (NIV).

Outward, pretend happiness covers up the fact that these individuals are struggling internally and sabotaging any real relationship with other people and with the Lord. In a way, it's easier to love others—or at least to appear to do so—than to love ourselves. I question if we can truly love other people in the way Jesus wants us to, with grace, compassion, and forgiveness, if we don't know how to love ourselves. When we say to ourselves, "Nobody loves me," it's dangerous to our mental and spiritual health. It's not only self-deprecation, but a lie the enemy tells us with the intention of keeping Christ's children from His true love.

I challenge people who have embraced this lie to explore their understanding of what Jesus meant by His teachings in the Gospels, such as the command to "love your neighbor as yourself" (Mark 12:31 NIV). The golden rule is important, but it's not only about treating others well. I ask people, "If you're showing love to someone, would you say to that person the things you say to yourself?"

They are appalled because, of course, they would never say aloud to other people the harsh things they tell themselves. Why not? They tell me that doing so would be disrespectful and socially unacceptable. "I wouldn't want to hurt their feelings," they point out.

If you do as Scripture instructs and love your neighbor as you love yourself, you must be speaking to the people around you in an unkind and critical, even hostile, manner. If that's the case, I wouldn't want to be your neighbor, as you would be the person hanging out of your window, constantly criticizing me and hurling insults in my direction.

If it's not okay to act that way and say hurtful words to your neighbor, then why is it okay to treat yourself so unlovingly? Most of us were socialized to believe that if we love ourselves, then we're conceited and self-absorbed and think that we're better than other people. We're indoctrinated in the idea that other people are better than we are. Putting others' needs ahead of ours can be good, but not if we're dismissing our own critical needs to focus entirely on other people.

I need to be clear: I don't believe that Christ was telling us to be self-absorbed, but He also wasn't saying that we should hate ourselves. The very idea of loving your neighbor as yourself assumes that you love yourself! However, we live in a world that attempts to steal our self-love and sense of self-worth, and we often end up focusing on the negative. When we constantly evaluate ourselves in a harsh light, it interferes with our ability to treat others well and show the love Christ intends for His people to demonstrate. He said, "By this everyone will know that you are my disciples, if you love one another" (John 13:35 NIV).

THE CHURCH'S ROLE

Sadly, the very body of believers that should provide love and support for Christians who are in pain too often fails in that role by reinforcing a poor understanding of Scripture.

Often the church teaches that if you have depression or a severe form of anxiety, it's your fault. You're not praying enough, or your faith is lacking. This view sends the message that depression is sin or an indication of sin, perhaps even God's judgment for sinful behaviors or laziness.

You can see how this message is terribly shame-inducing for people who are trying to manage negative emotions that they don't want and would gladly rid themselves of. I like to say, "Church would be great without the folks," because the folks—myself included—show up with their unique personalities, attitudes, joys, worries, and conflicts. The people who come to church often fear the expression of their feelings unless those feelings are all positive.

Refusal to deal with or even acknowledge the negative emotions people experience is alienating and only heightens the struggle. People who are depressed are already grappling with their self-worth, and dismissive or accusatory messages from the church and other Christians may affirm their belief that they aren't good enough and result in increased feelings of guilt and shame. It's important to differentiate between the two. Guilt tells you that you have *done* something wrong, but shame says that *you* are wrong.

As much as I believe in the power of prayer and seeking the Lord's rescue for people who are experiencing depression or anxiety, I also believe that He provides us with the resources to help us process those emotions. I would never tell someone, "Just pray about it, and it will be fine," or any of the other clichéd responses that do harm to those wrestling with depression, such as:

- "Just get over it."
- "Stop feeling sorry for yourself."
- "Think about other people who have it worse."
- "What do you have to be sad about?"
- "I know what you're feeling, and I got through it, so anyone can."
- "You must have unconfessed sin in your life."

I could go on and on with the things non-depressed people should never say to someone who is depressed.

Several years ago, I had a client who was dealing with a chronic depressed mood. This woman's fear and shame were visible. Every week, she would sit as far away from me in my small office as she could. I'm not exaggerating. Her chair was actually gouging holes into the drywall from her trying to push it farther away from me. I wondered why she kept returning on a weekly basis if fear had such a solid grip on her.

Over time, we built a rapport, and I helped her to understand the process of therapy, including the addition of medication as approved by her doctor. After a while, she revealed some factors that contributed to her depression, and they had much to do with her belief system.

She believed that she was "full of sin" and "didn't have enough faith," and, as a result, was not worthy of being healed from depression. She saw taking antidepressants and going to therapy as marks of weakness, and she was ashamed of both. These weren't feelings that had appeared from nowhere and lodged in her mind. The very church that should have been supporting her and lifting her up in prayer before God had taken the wrong approach to helping her through her mental illness.

At first glance, it would seem that the church elders were trying their best to help. They would gather in a circle, with this woman in the middle, and pray over her. After all, God's Word tells us in James 5:14, "Is anyone among you sick? Let them call the elders of the church to pray over them and anoint them with oil in the name of the Lord" (NIV). However, my client admitted that they did this not in a spirit of love and understanding, but in condemnation.

They couldn't understand what was deemed "her resistance" to healing. It was as if they thought she chose to be depressed. In their minds, prayer should be an instant fix, but instead of being miraculously cured, this woman would walk away from these prayer interventions feeling worse—more depressed and more anxious—than before.

She thought that it was "just her" and believed that, because of the lack of improvement, she must not be worth the Lord's healing, so she denied herself any comfort that should come from prayer. She thought that she was too full of sin. She even believed that she would be better off dead. A group of well-meaning church folks had sabotaged her attempts at healing through a legalistic approach that pointed her away from God and toward self-destruction.

This again highlights the church's resistance to dealing with negative emotions, which stands in stark contrast to what Scripture tells us. Numerous individuals throughout the Bible were dragged into the valley of dry bones, just as my client was. King David lamented, "My guilt has overwhelmed me like a burden too heavy to bear" (Psalm 38:4 NIV). Moses begged, "If this is how you are going to treat me, please go ahead and kill me—if I have found favor in your eyes—and do not let me face my own ruin" (Numbers 11:15 NIV). Even Christ told His disciples, "My soul is overwhelmed with sorrow to the point of death" (Matthew 26:38 NIV).

Did God condemn them for their anguish? No, He didn't. He met them where they were to minister to their pain and bring them to healing.

When it came to this particular client, I wondered if she could be dealing with a chemical imbalance or if there was actually a sinful response at play. It turned out to be both, though not in the way you may think.

For starters, she did have a chemical imbalance, which medication alleviated. It took her some time to agree to the medication because—back to her belief system—she said that it was wrong to rely on it and she should simply trust the Lord.

I brought up the fact that she wore glasses. "Why do you wear them?" I asked.

She gave me a funny look. "Um, so I can see."

"So, what happens if you don't wear them?"

"I run into things."

"Well, then, it sounds like you've made a choice to wear them."

"No, there is no choice, because if I don't wear them, then I could hurt myself and other people."

"Here's the thing: we tend to accept medical conditions

like the need to wear glasses, diabetes, high blood pressure, and even obesity as physical ailments or conditions, but we don't see depression this way. That's the reason why you view not being able to heal from depression as a lack of faith but wearing glasses as a necessity to improve your faith. Otherwise, wearing glasses could be a sign of the same supposed lack of faith."

This realization helped her to change her thinking, and as we talked more, she also gained insight into her victim mentality. While her inability to heal from depression wasn't sinful, her response to her emotions might have been. There was a secondary gain: to have others feel sorry for her situation. This kept her from developing meaningful relationships and gave her an excuse to have other people tell her what to do. She developed learned helplessness, which was preventing her from becoming the empowered woman God intended her to be.

This awareness, coupled with the medication that treated chemical imbalances, lifted her from the depressed state. She gained confidence to set appropriate boundaries and use assertive communication. She opened her heart to God's favor over her life. She continued to heal, but not without occasionally relapsing into old patterns of thought, behavior, and coping. It seemed to me that the times she would regress would be when she was condemned for the progress she was making. What we do serves a purpose for us, but it also serves a purpose for others. Her progress did not serve the purpose of her church elders.

I often wondered what motive they had for wanting her

to stay stuck. Was it because their attempts at prayer hadn't led to the miraculous healing they wanted? Had their expectations been subverted? Was their pride wounded? The most important part of her journey was remembering that Jesus came to set the captives free (Luke 4:14–21). Here was a group of individuals who should have been fulfilling His work on the earth but were instead pulling a woman back into captivity.

RECONNECTING

Often people who are suffering from depression don't realize that they're withdrawing. They start disconnecting from other people, and as that disconnection deepens, it makes the situation worse. They think that nobody likes them. Nobody wants to hang out with them. They begin to believe that they're unworthy, so they withdraw even further.

I spent a lot of my early years feeling disposable, like I could be easily tossed aside, especially when compared to other things that I thought were much more important. This is where the primary feeling of insignificance was birthed. I believed that I could be tossed away, so I acted like I had been tossed away, as if embracing the inevitability of rejection and failure. This was accompanied by the desperate inner cry of "No, no, please don't toss me away!" It was a brutal cycle.

It was a long road to get where I am today. I didn't simply show up on scene, knowing what I know now, without stumbles. A lot of self-examination and prayer was involved. I had to get to the point where I realized that I wasn't actually disposable in those relationships. That was a belief I had about myself, like my client's belief that she was too sinful to be healed. It was very difficult for me to accept that I was who the Lord said I was—that is, that my identity came from my relationship with Christ and not from my relationships with other people.

I can never forget that the Lord is there to lead me out of the valley of dry bones. His is the voice prophesying over me in the wilderness, and I can put my hope in Him as I tackle difficulties like depression. It won't let me go easily, but if I seek the help He provides and banish the lie of the enemy that I'm not worth saving, His voice will guide me free. He will guide you, too, because you are worth saving!

WORKBOOK

Chapter Four Questions

Question: Do you know anyone who has depression? Were you surprised when you found out? Why or why not?

I suspect marc does but likely he doesn't realize or admit it.

Question: How can you support friends and family members who struggle with depression or anxiety? How can you encourage your church community to do the same?

Education, listening well, being open + honest @ my own issues / struggles.

Question: Are you currently experiencing any of the signs of depression outlined in this chapter? If so, what steps can you begin taking to seek and accept help?

_____
_____
_____
_____
_____
_____

Action: Make a list of the things you tell yourself that you wouldn't say to someone you love. Next to each one, write one or more scriptures that challenge the unloving statement.

P. 61-62 I can relate + I think ADD is often viewed + experienced the same way.
Painful on the inside + ~~fine~~ on the outside.
P. 69 - Guilt -vs- Shame - defined

Chapter Four Notes

CHAPTER FIVE

Living with Grief and What It Can Teach Us

Lazarus was dead. His sisters were in shock. Christ came to them and made a radical, astonishing promise: their brother would live again. It was unheard of and, to them, might have seemed arrogant.

Before He got to the miracle, before He showed how He could breathe new life into dead, dry bones, Jesus and His disciples arrived at the burial site. What follows is perhaps the shortest verse in all of Scripture: "Jesus wept" (John 11:35).

Our Savior, who was fully man and fully God, knew what it was to feel loss. Could this have been His first experience of the death of a loved one during His time on the earth? Surely not, given the short life spans of that period and the threats to health and life from every angle. But in the two words of that verse, we're exposed to the reality that even Jesus was affected by grief.

What do you think of when you hear the word *grief*? Most

people probably think of a loved one dying and might picture a funeral, with everyone dressed in black and gathered under umbrellas beside the grave while a pastor reads a sermon. We equate grief with loss, and it's true that there's nothing as heart-wrenching as the loss we experience when someone we love dies. But we grieve over all manner of things that we've lost, including friendships, jobs, a church home, or even the ability to enjoy an activity that's suddenly beyond our reach for health or financial reasons.

Grief is the normal response to a loss. It's strong and overwhelming. There's no denying its power, even if it's in response to what other people might think is trivial. It often comes in a single moment that punches us in the gut and leaves us reeling.

You might have heard people reference the five stages of grief, which were first formulated by Elisabeth Kübler-Ross in 1969.[11] Her book *On Death and Dying* has defined how we think about and categorize the experience of grief for more than half a century. Those five stages of grief are:

- Denial
- Anger
- Bargaining
- Depression
- Acceptance

This describes our individual experiences of grief, but there's also such a thing as communal grief. Think about what we've all experienced through the course of the recent pandemic, with the loss of life, loss of social connections, loss of jobs and businesses. Not only that, but we've also witnessed and experienced social upheaval, mass shootings, and increased division due to political tensions. It's taken years to work toward recovery, but the process of grief isn't always recognized by society. Nobody has really talked about that kind of recovery.

It's fair to say that society in general doesn't deal with grief well, even though we see funerals all the time. There are people who feel ashamed or condemned for taking a natural amount of time to grieve a death. Others may ask them insensitive, brutal questions, like "That's still a problem for you? Didn't he die six months ago?" Some may even say, "Don't keep talking about it. It's a downer to everyone else."

GRIEF IS PERSONAL AND UNIQUE

I had a client who had just moved to the area with her husband. They hadn't even unpacked all their boxes into their new retirement home at the beach. They were done with the career phase of their life and were ready to enjoy everything retirement promised. Doesn't that sound like a great thing?

Imagine my surprise when this woman (I'll call her Rachel) showed up for a session with me, overwhelmed and in shock. She told me that everything was fine one moment, and then the next, her husband was dead. He had a heart attack.

It's difficult to imagine yourself in Rachel's shoes. How must it have felt to be standing at the edge of this new part of their lives together when, suddenly, he was gone? My client couldn't wrap her head around his absence.

I started out by simply listening to her and validating how difficult it was. This offered her a space to feel what she was feeling. So many times, people ask, "Am I doing this right? Is this what I'm supposed to feel? Is this normal?" Once they hear that it's okay, relief floods them.

Grief is personal and unique. Not everyone needs to hear the same things. Most often, you need to let people know that they are experiencing ordinary emotions in response to extraordinary events. This type of reassurance helps grieving individuals to feel more "normal."

People often experience disenfranchised grief, which is a fancy way of saying that they grieve alone. Disenfranchised grief is when there is a loss that's not recognized, such as the loss of a pet or a relationship. Perhaps your oldest child has moved out. A mother could have lost a child through miscarriage or sought an abortion. Even dementia is a form of loss.

What happens in these cases is that the loss is either not recognized or not valued. Grieving alone can result in silent grief if the person who has experienced the loss feels the need to hide or suppress his or her emotions in order to avoid causing other people to feel uncomfortable.

Some people then push the grief far away from themselves and remain in that first phase. Denial can initially help us to survive the loss; that much is true. Denial is our shock and disbelief about what has just happened. Our brains are trying to make sense of the loss, and it's overwhelming, so we go into a numb state or attempt to live in a preferred reality. "It can't be true" or "I don't believe it" are some things we may say.

We start looking for evidence that the loss is not real. We don't accept it, and that actually helps to pace the impact of the loss for us until we're able to handle it.

Even as we're denying that there has been a tremendous loss, we still go through the motions, such as funeral arrangements. It's strange how we can program ourselves to avoid acknowledging the loss while taking the steps that will end with our loved one's funeral, but what we're really doing is suppressing the emotions bubbling up inside of us. Once we start to accept the loss, we feel the impact, and the healing can begin.

When Rachel's husband died soon after they retired, I guided her through talking about her husband and the circumstances surrounding his death. This wasn't a single question with an easy answer. We had to experience what she was feeling several times while she recounted the event. This helped Rachel to integrate what happened and to recognize that the loss was real. We then discussed strategies for returning to work and managing upcoming events, such as the Year of the Firsts—the first time going to the grocery store without him, the first Christmas without him, and so forth.

I gave her grief education to help her understand what to expect, such as how grief comes and goes, rises and falls. We think of those five stages of grief as steps that should proceed sequentially, when in reality, they exist on a continuum. "We tend to ebb and flow through these states," Kübler-Ross wrote. "They are like waves and come take us under the riptide of emotion when we least expect it."[12]

My client had to struggle against that riptide. There was

no easy check-off-the box method for her to use as she grappled with her emotions. With her husband's death, she had lost many things. She had lost her lifestyle—going on a boating excursion with her husband or taking a long trip together. She'd lost the father of her children. She'd lost financial stability. She'd lost the person with whom she could talk things through. She'd lost the idea of what a good retirement life was like.

In order to process her grief over everything she had lost, she needed each of the individual losses to be acknowledged, validated, and normalized. She admitted to struggling with how people "just went on with their lives" and expected her to be strong. It was hard for her not to talk about her husband, but she could see that every time she did, people became uncomfortable, so she suppressed her hurt. Because she allowed herself to express her hurt in the session with me, stayed focused on Jesus, and maintained her faith, she was able to work through the pain and adjust to a new normal for her life. She didn't fully get over her grief, but the intensity of the emotion lessened.

In other cases, people come in for a session to talk about their depression, but after some discussion, I'll point out, "Well, this sounds like you're experiencing grief." Often they don't realize that they are mourning a loss. It's not a matter of denial, but a lack of recognition.

Many people retire in my neck of the woods, like my client who tragically lost her husband. Have you ever been on vacation and thought, "Wow, wouldn't it be great to live here instead of just visiting?" I certainly have. It sounds good, but people find out that reality has a far greater impact than fantasy.

Some people decide to move to a place where they have vacationed for years. But when they get there and are living there, they find that it's not a vacation anymore; it's different. They're experiencing more of a day-to-day existence than new adventures every day. The reality doesn't measure up to the fantasy, and that can be a difficult adjustment to make.

Add to this the fact that they've left everything that was part of their day-to-day lives for several decades: their former neighborhood, their former community, longtime friends. These changes impact them so greatly that they're unable to keep up their motivation and they find themselves saying, "I think I'm homesick."

Eventually, I end up drawing out of them the reality that they're dealing with grief over the multiple losses they've experienced. What they're feeling is completely normal, but they don't see it that way because, frankly, no one died. They don't give themselves permission to grieve because they don't understand that it's possible to grieve the loss of friendships, pets, and situations. They may even feel self-conscious about it, telling me, "I thought it was kind of silly because I chose to move here," or "We decided to come here as a couple, and now I'm all upset. That doesn't seem to make sense. What's wrong with me?"

At this point, they do recognize that they're in grief, so they're not denying the emotion. Rather, they're trying to hide from it instead of confronting it head-on. The ways in which people react to their grief, no matter what kind it is, vary greatly. There isn't any one way that's right or wrong, unless we're talking about harmful behaviors.

Like with most other struggles and difficulties, many people respond to grief in unhealthy ways, such as:

- Self-medicating with drugs, alcohol, food, shopping, or anything else they can use as a distraction
- Rushing into another relationship or getting another pet to try to replace the lost relationship
- Avoiding talking about the loss and avoiding places that may trigger the loss
- Minimizing the loss or "Christianizing" it by relying on platitudes instead of problem-solving
- Becoming too busy or overly involved with other activities
- Isolating or withdrawing from other people and activities

It's reactions like these that highlight why it's so important to process our emotions, including grief, and find opportunities to talk about them. One of the situations that's most difficult is the one in which you would think it would be most natural to deal with grief: a funeral.

Funerals are as much a part of our lives as weddings. Millions of people attend them every day, yet we have a lot of difficulty with them in our society. We don't all handle them the same way. I've seen everything from people wailing and falling across the coffin to people joking, laughing, and carrying on as if they're at a party. The people who make outward displays of extreme grief tend to have a negative effect on other mourners. Keep in mind that I'm not passing judgment on them. I've heard those other mourners grumble, "They just need to quit it." Why is that? Well, it's because people are generally uncomfortable with other people's emotions, especially grief.

On the other hand, I've heard complaints when some of the mourners appear to be having a good time. Other people will comment, "I don't know why they're doing that. Their loved one is lying in that coffin, and they're having a party in front of them!"

In some ways, the people who complain about either of those extreme examples are having a harder time processing their own emotions than the people who choose the bold outward expressions of grief. People are trying to navigate their own feelings. It's an uncomfortable experience to discuss or even acknowledge grief, and it's uncomfortable to be at a funeral.

I try to be mindful of the grieving family and follow their lead. I make sure to ask them, "How are you doing?" or "Are you well right now?" The customary expression that people tend to offer those who have recently lost a loved one—"I'm sorry for your loss"—is simply not helpful.

More often than not, the bereaved are in such a fog that they're not going to remember exactly what you say to them. Rather, they'll remember what it felt like when you were there with them. If you say, "I'm sorry for your loss," that makes it more about you than about them and their loss.

We need to be present for the bereaved and talk to them about what's really going on: the loss. They're grieving, and it's important to acknowledge that. For example, I may say, "This is really hard." It's more important to choose our words carefully and try to offer the grieving individuals a chance to begin processing their loss than it is for us to say the easiest thing possible so we can quickly extricate ourselves from a situation we find uncomfortable. Again, if we're not the ones suffering the loss of a loved one, then it's not about us.

JOB'S FRIENDS AND FAMILY

Discussing loss and grief brings to mind another classic portrayal of grief in Scripture. When you think of someone in the Bible who suffered great loss, you may jump right to Job. He did suffer and, for the most part, suffered well—the people around him, not so much.

His wife had a difficult time with her losses and ended up telling Job to "curse God and die" (Job 2:9 NKJV). She was saying to him, "You should just give up! What's the point?" She was hurting and trying to process her own grief. She couldn't make it better, and the person who had provided her with the things she had lost couldn't fix it, either. It's likely that she was ebbing and flowing through the stages of grief.

Think about all they had lost. In telling this Bible story, we often say that Job's children died, but they were his wife's children, too. Those were her babies who were suddenly taken from her forever. Her emotions must have been overwhelming, and she might have held Job responsible for her children's deaths. We try to make meaning from our losses. Her outrage might have been something she could cling to, or she might have thought, "Everything else has been taken from me. Why not you, too? I won't be able to handle losing you later, but if you go now, it may not be as hard on me."

Then we meet Job's three friends. They knew that he was suffering, and they initially did the right things. They offered empathy and spent time with him. They held space for him, as we discussed earlier. However, after seven days, apparently enough was enough. Job didn't get over his grief quickly, so they started giving him speeches. These supposed friends blamed Job for his suffering. They accused him of unrepented sin and encouraged him to admit his wrongdoing so God would bless him again.

I wonder if they really wanted Job to be blessed again or if they simply wanted to get on with their lives. They had come to comfort him and to grieve with him, but they were tired of it and wanted things to get better for Job and for themselves. It's like when the church elders prayed over my client who was depressed and then were upset with her when she wasn't instantly and miraculously cured. Some things never change. Not seeing any improvement in Job's condition might have been a blow to their egos or a test of their patience, so they started making speeches.

Job called them "miserable comforters" (Job 16:2 NKJV), and I cannot disagree. Even after he critiqued them to their faces, they continued to berate him and give him advice instead of comfort. None of his friends had gone through the level of tragic loss that Job had suffered. They couldn't relate. They couldn't wrap their heads around it. It was overwhelming. Regardless, their insensitivity in blaming Job for his suffering and implying that he had cast his children into hell is difficult to swallow. How could Job's grief-stricken heart bear such hurtful words?

From another perspective, I wonder if Job's friends had experienced their own losses and didn't know how to manage their grief. Were they uncomfortable with what Job's grief brought up in themselves? Many times, our unmanaged grief gets in the way of us being truly present with others. We take the opportunity to say, "That happened to me, too," or we remain in a place of denial and avoid the emotion.

Even in the darkest of times, the Lord is never far off. He responded sternly to Job's three friends, saying, "My wrath is aroused against you and your two friends, for you have not spoken of Me what is right, as My servant Job has" (Job 42:7 NKJV).

FINDING GOD IN GRIEF

What does God have to say to us about grief? It turns out that Scripture has plenty to reveal to us on the subject, even though it seems like we skim over those verses when we're not experiencing loss.

We've already looked at Job and Jesus, but you may remember that our Lord also grieved a loss He was about to experience when He prayed in the garden of Gethsemane. He was distraught over His imminent death. He prayed three times—not once, but three times—that the "cup" of what He was about to suffer would be taken away (Matthew 26:36–44). However, each time, He immediately deferred to His Father's will. The emotions of Jesus' human nature were in turmoil. These emotions are so powerful that even our Savior was overcome by them in that moment.

Scripture also offers encouragement for those who grieve. Consider the following verses:

Blessed are those who mourn, for they shall be comforted.
*—**Matthew 5:4** (ESV)*

He will wipe away every tear from their eyes, and death shall be no more, neither shall there be mourning, nor crying, nor pain anymore, for the former things have passed away.
*—**Revelation 21:4** (ESV)*

Blessed are you who are hungry now, for you shall be satisfied. Blessed are you who weep now, for you shall laugh.
*—**Luke 6:21** (ESV)*

For I consider that the sufferings of this present time are not worth comparing with the glory that is to be revealed to us.
*—**Romans 8:18** (ESV)*

None of these verses are meant to minimize grief. Rather, they show that God knows what we're dealing with and always stands ready to comfort His children.

So, from a practical standpoint, what can we do? How do we deal with our grief, especially when it can be difficult to find someone to talk to about such a deep and powerful emotion? Much of what needs to happen involves self-compassion and the building of resilience in ourselves.

It's okay to miss the person you loved. You can feel bad about it. You don't have to remain emotionally tied up and never say anything to anyone else. Give yourself permission.

How? Give yourself permission through journaling and counseling. Give yourself permission to participate in organizations like GriefShare or Compassionate Friends, which provide a support network of people who have also sustained loss. Allow yourself to see that you're not in this by yourself. God's Word tells us not to forsake the gathering of the saints (Hebrews 10:25). You are not only allowed, but encouraged, to come together with other people of a similar and familiar mindset. You need to give yourself permission, and you need to give other grieving people permission as well.

In my practice, I often find it helpful to provide an environment for people to give themselves permission simply to feel their feelings. People don't always allow themselves to feel their emotions. Perhaps they don't even want to feel; they don't want to cry. But even Jesus wept. The Father was there for Him, and He is here for you.

WORKBOOK

Chapter Five Questions

Question: Have you ever experienced grief over a loss other than the death of a loved one? Were you able to identify your emotions as stemming from grief? How did this affect how you reacted to and handled the loss?

Ebenezer courses: Loss List - Timeline - revealed underlying issue of "powerlessness."

1996 - I dealt w/ it terribly + suffered for it.

2104 + 2021 - God is walking it out w/ me + I am flourishing.
* But - now little holiday season + yesterday as I watched the UMD football game my heart

is heavy + sad for Marc. I grieve the loss of the Marc I knew for the 2 years we dated. Even in all the "vetting" we did + it was substantial, he was faking all of us out. I'm sad because I don't see "improvement" in the near future. I fear I cannot live with or even be around.

Question: When you witness other people grieve, what emotions are triggered in you? How do you speak and act as a result?

It often stirs my past losses but when I do it well, I just "sit with it" or sit with them. – Elena + Monique –

myself: I allow time to "feel" but within a healthy routine that keeps my balance and keeps me moving forward. Always "forward" leading toward "home," heaven, Christ.

Question: What has helped you most in times when you were grieving?

Relationships – God, people, work connection, fitness, peace + quiet. Home + pets, health. Laughter.

Action: If you are experiencing grief right now, give yourself permission to feel what you are feeling. Consider tools and opportunities that may help you to process your grief, such as journaling, counseling, and connecting with a support network of other people experiencing loss. If you know someone who is grieving, help that person to know that he or she is allowed to feel. Give this person a safe environment for talking about his or her emotions. Offer comfort without judgment, remembering that grief is unique to each individual.

Cognitive distortions -

Chapter Five Notes

grief - loss, emptiness, a void where something/someone once was -

- I want to travel again w/ great friends.
- 70% of "presenting" anger issues turn out to be unresolved grief / loss.

★ I believed it was all up to me.

CHAPTER SIX

Anger Management and Emotional Self-Regulation

We like to get angry. Of all the emotions we deal with, anger is perhaps the most satisfying. Who hasn't felt that surge of satisfaction when becoming angry or venting frustration? Expressing our anger offers us a measure of control often lacking in the rest of our lives.

The COVID-19 pandemic had a huge impact on our lives and our mental health. At the beginning, with all the lockdowns, I didn't go out a lot. Even later, I still didn't go out, mostly because I didn't have to. When I did finally start reintroducing myself into the world, I'd drive somewhere and notice what I considered to be the bad driving all around me. You can imagine me in my car: "Oh, is this how we're doing it now? Seriously? We're just cutting in front of people? Must be a new way of driving. I didn't know they took away your turn signal during the pandemic!"

I was expressing my anger at a situation I didn't like. I'm

thankful that I was the only one in my car and no one else heard me!

Anger can be an important tool when it helps us to identify our passions. We harness it to call out injustice and fight for those who are downtrodden. Anger can also protect us from danger.

However, anger is perhaps the most destructive emotion we can unleash on those around us. We use it to hurt the people we love the most. Like with many other emotions, we misuse the tool given to us. Why, then, is anger management not dealt with more seriously among believers?

I suspect that, among the Lord's people, anger isn't seen as much of a danger because of a misapplication of Scripture. Anger is okay if it's considered what we call "righteous anger." I'm sure you've heard it preached before. Jesus displayed His righteous anger when He flipped the money changers' tables as they were conducting business in the temple courts using shady practices (Matthew 21:12–13; Mark 11:15–17; Luke 19:45–46; John 2:13–17).

Our references to righteous anger can be warped if we don't have a clear definition of what it means. We may end up twisting it to our own selfish purposes. Who decides what counts as righteous anger for me or for you? As I'm sure you know, there are many interpretations of what Scripture says regarding what goes against God's will. If I determine, based on my church experience, that something is against what God wants, then I may wield anger as a weapon against it. Paul cautioned us that we should be angry and not sin (Ephesians 4:26–27), but I think that it becomes easy to deny or justify the sin part if we tell ourselves that most, if not all, of our anger is righteous anger against the things of which God doesn't approve.

ACKNOWLEDGING ANGER

The emotion of anger is so accepted in our society that often we don't recognize it to be a problem. To bring awareness to anger, it's helpful to have a deliberate approach when talking about it. It's not as simple as saying, "You're angry, so you need to do something about it."

The gut reaction of the person you're addressing will often be: "How do you know what I'm feeling?"

Then you reply, "Well, I know you, so I know you're angry. Of course, you're angry."

While your observation may be correct, it doesn't offer the person an environment in which he or she feels safe enough to be vulnerable, talk through the emotions, and make a change.

What has worked for me is helping people to use their words differently. I start out by listening and making observations. Then I'll say, "Gosh, this feels to me like anger. Is it? Does it feel that way to you? I'm getting the sense that something is going on."

This is a gentle way to start the conversation. Like the example I gave in Chapter Two of communicating with my coworker, it puts the focus on the behavior, not the person. It's also a helpful base to build on. The person typically responds, "No, I'm not angry." That's when I can come back with, "Okay, when I see X, Y, and Z, I interpret that as anger, but thank you for telling me that it's not. Can you share with me what is going on? Is there something else?"

I should point out that anger management is the only therapy in which I work with groups rather than individuals. There's something amazing about this gathering of people who are struggling with anger. After weeks of meeting together, I see them walk out of the bondage of anger and blame. They're able to say, "Okay, I get it," and they become champions of the process themselves.

Some of my anger management group participants are voluntary, those who are already my clients or are seeing other therapists, but most are either "highly recommended" or court ordered to be there. Before people can register for the group, they have to meet with me for an intake assessment so I can determine whether or not joining the group is appropriate for them and what their level of insight is regarding their anger.

Typically, *denial* is the word of the day. I hear a lot of "I'm not angry" and "I don't know why I have to come to this [expletive deleted] class." My first task is to lay out the group's procedure and the criteria the participants must fulfill if they want to receive their certificate of completion. That doesn't put a stop to the grumbling, and when the time comes for our first sessions together, there are inevitably a few people who come in figuratively kicking and screaming. Even as adults—perhaps especially as adults—we don't like being told what to do.

One gentleman stands out in my memory. He was ordered

Anger Management and Emotional Self-Regulation

by his employer to attend anger management therapy. Let's call him Johnny, after Johnny Lawrence, an antagonist in the *Karate Kid*.[13] That's a whole different level of anger issues! At least this situation didn't involve martial arts.

Johnny was one of those people who was sure that he already knew everything. He reminded me of the students who sit at the back of the classroom and do their best to ignore the lesson being taught from the front while also derailing their classmates' attention. You know the kind of kid I mean. He would be the one mocking the teacher, laughing at his own jokes, and initiating conflict with his fellow students.

I did have an advantage in that I met Johnny before the class began, which meant that I was prepared in advance for this kind of disruptive behavior. This particular group only had seven people, so I set up the chairs in the room without a back row and put Johnny to the right of me. You may think it's funny that I, in a physical sense, made him my right-hand man, even though that position is one we equate with trust and reliability. I placed Johnny in this position because I wanted to speak to his left brain, which, according to multiple studies, is dominant when it comes to processing positive comments.[14] It also tends to be analytical.

Once we got started, I could see Johnny's standard mode of operation emerging. Sometimes he would initiate arguments. At other times, he would try to align with me by putting down the other participants, but always on the sly. The common thread in these various behaviors was his insistence on minimizing his anger.

When I host these sessions, somewhere around the third

group meeting, generally speaking, the participants begin to form a level of cohesion and experience flashes of emotional insight. Johnny's group was no different. Their defensive denial started to shift because the group process allowed them to be vulnerable and transparent. Once participants began developing these healthier attitudes and behaviors, they started calling Johnny out on his lack of growth and pushed him to participate actively in the process.

Johnny started acknowledging his anger instead of pushing it aside and was able to identify the primary emotion motivating it. He no longer denied that he was experiencing and exhibiting this negative side of his emotions. His insights into his anger-influenced behaviors surprised him, and he developed better skills for dealing with anger when it started to heat up.

By the time we reached the end of our twelve-week session, Johnny was no longer the defiant "I don't have an anger problem" person who sat there with his jaw clenched and his arms crossed. Instead, he became an advocate for the very process in which he'd been forced to participate. He would announce to the group, "Everyone should come to this!" He admitted he had gained so much that he didn't want his participation to end.

Johnny's realization that his anger had crossed over from being a good tool used in managing difficult situations to being a harmful aspect of his personality changed not only his mindset, but also how he lived his day-to-day life.

I saw Johnny in a grocery store about a year later. I should mention here that as a professional standard for myself, I don't speak to a client in public unless the client speaks to me first. At first, I didn't recognize Johnny, but once we greeted each other, we weren't client and licensed professional counselor, but simply two people getting their meat and cheese. This particular deli counter was slow, and the customers passed the time by making small talk. Johnny took full advantage of the opportunity to launch into his experiences using his newfound anger management skills.

Johnny categorized himself as a "large and in-charge" kind of guy. That part of his personality hadn't changed since attending the group sessions, but he now used it for good instead of ill, telling everyone who would listen about the anger management sessions and how he had wrongly assumed that he didn't need that kind of help.

DEALING WITH ANGER

So, what kind of shift do we need to undergo in order to get a handle on our anger? The key, as with many other situations in our lives, is taking responsibility. First, we must recognize that no one can *make* us feel a certain way.

Do you recall my story about turning into an upset driver when I started getting out of the house again after the pandemic lockdown? Many people would probably look at that situation and say, "Well, sure, those other drivers made you angry with their bad driving!" That's the kind of unhelpful thinking that strips away our responsibility.

Other people can invite, influence, impact, or even provoke our emotions, but we are in charge of regulating our onses. If we can first recognize and acknowledge our poor regulation of our anger, we can then identify the primary emotional triggers that set off the emotion and build better strategies for handling those events.

==Anger, anxiety, and depression are se==condary emotions. Primary emotions are those that we feel beforehand, such as ==guilt, shame, embarrassment, rejection, betrayal, or abandonment.== We tend to feel vulnerable when we experience those primary emotions. We don't want other people to know those aspects of us, because we believe (probably based on personal experience) that they might use our vulnerabilities against us. In an effort to protect ourselves from others and perhaps even from ourselves, we either push out in anger or pull in through anxiety or depression. We cannot change anything if we don't first acknowledge those primary emotional triggers.

Our culture embraces anger. I would argue that it even makes anger necessary. Don't you get messages to that effect all the time? We may hear, "You'll get what you want if you get angry," or the milder version: "The squeaky wheel gets the grease."

This starts, as most things do, when we are children. Adults and peers socialize us in what I'd term "poor anger." For example, boys are supposed to be more aggressive than girls and, by extension, embrace anger in the way society deems best. Parents and other adults may tell them, "Don't take that kind of nonsense from someone!" or "Get in there and get them!" Boys are told to act out in anger.

On the contrary, girls are socialized to be passive around

everyone. They're bombarded with messages such as "don't act ugly" and "be nice." Never mind the more complicated "What will your friends say?" and "People won't like you." These constant reminders lead girls to suppress not only their anger, even healthy expressions of it, but other negative emotions as well.

Both of these sets of messaging raise children into adults who do the same thing. Spread that across the nation, and we wind up with a society full of people who are ill-equipped for emotional regulation. Judging by how they learned these poor habits as children, they will pass them on to the next generation, believing that it's simply how things are done. This is how we pass down the valley of dry bones from generation to generation as we talked about in Chapter One.

Again, the key is to remember that no one else is controlling our behaviors. Changing our thoughts and feelings subsequently changes the accompanying behavior, empowering us not to allow our reactions to be governed by outside influences. If someone says, "They pushed my buttons," I say, "Well, move your buttons."

Proverbs 1:17 tells us that if birds see a trap being set, they will stay away. In other words, the birds will go another way to avoid a trap if they know that it's there. The next verse goes on to say that people set ambushes for themselves by not paying attention. We need to start paying attention to what's happening with our own thoughts, emotions, and behaviors and begin developing healthy ways to cope.

It should be no surprise that, as with other negative feelings, we tend to shift blame for our anger. We say that someone else made us angry. We can see examples of this all the way back to Genesis. Adam's first response when God confronted him about eating the forbidden fruit was to try to shift blame. He tried to blame the woman for giving him the fruit and God for giving him the woman (Genesis 3:11–12). We see the generational fallout when Adam's son Cain killed his other son, Abel. Cain played coy when God asked him where Abel was, replying, "I don't know.... Am I my brother's keeper?" (Genesis 4:9 NIV).

Individuals with limited emotional insight may recognize that they have a problem with their anger, but they won't take responsibility for it. Instead, they talk about the situations and people that somehow force them to become angry.

It seems that this problem has only intensified over the last decade or so. Our society is full of people who are easily offended by every little thing and want others to take responsibility for the way they're feeling. There's a desire, whether conscious or unconscious, to stay in the victim's role when it comes to emotions. We need to consider better ways to manage what we're feeling, and that begins with owning our angry reactions and understanding our primary emotions.

Consider Nehemiah. In chapter 5 of the book that bears his name, we find Nehemiah upset because the people of Israel, newly resettled in the promised land after the Babylonian exile, came to him with a pile of complaints. They dumped them all right at his feet. There were too many people, so they needed to get more grain so they wouldn't starve. They had to mortgage their fields and homes to get food.

They had to borrow money to pay off their taxes. They were powerless to prevent their daughters from being enslaved.

How did Nehemiah react? He wrote, "When I heard their outcry and these charges, I was very angry. I pondered them in my mind and then accused the nobles and officials" (Nehemiah 5:6 NIV). Nehemiah didn't lash out at the people complaining, even though what they were saying provoked his anger. Instead of snapping at people in an unproductive manner, he thought on it for a while and then made a strategic plan to change what was wrong and get justice for those who were suffering. He wasn't about to let corrupt officials oppress God's people! Nehemiah went before those leaders and pointed out that what they were doing to their own people was wrong. He demanded compassion and morally upright decisions. He was angry, but his anger wasn't out of control.

Think about what the Apostle Paul said when he appeared before King Agrippa toward the end of Acts. Paul said, "King Agrippa, I consider myself fortunate to stand before you today as I make my defense against all the accusations of the Jews" (Acts 26:2 NIV). The New King James Version renders Paul's words as: "I think myself happy" (Acts 26:2 NKJV).

How do we cultivate this attitude in ourselves? As I mentioned earlier, anger is part of the emotional toolbox the Lord gave us, but we tend to misuse it. Similarly, though people often misquote the Bible as stating that "money is the root of all evil," the verse actually warns that "the love of money is a root of all kinds of evil" (1 Timothy 6:10 NIV). Neither money nor anger is in itself wrong, but we have the potential to handle these things in a warped and sinful way.

Probably the most famous verse about anger is in Paul's letter to the Ephesians: "Be angry and do not sin; do not let the sun go down on your anger" (Ephesians 4:26 ESV). Paul was telling fellow believers to manage their behavior, warning against the unhealthy use of anger. Often the best management strategy is to identify the primary emotion that occurs before the anger. Discovering the root cause of anger can help us to make the changes necessary to avoid harmful behaviors.

One of the most helpful aspects of Paul's letters is that he not only told believers that something was wrong and needed to be changed, but followed through with practical ways to make the change. Take a look at how he handled the topic of anxiety in his message to the Philippians. Paul advised, "Be anxious for nothing, but in everything by prayer and supplication, with thanksgiving, let your requests be made known to God; and the peace of God, which surpasses all understanding, will guard your hearts and minds through Christ Jesus" (Philippians 4:6–7 NKJV).

Paul didn't simply say, "Stop worrying," and end the letter there. That wouldn't have been particularly helpful. Instead, he said that if we pray to God and let Him know what's bothering us, we won't be worried anymore.

Practical Matters

I've talked a lot about the situations surrounding anger and the way other people have handled the reformation of their emotional management, but what about you? There are plenty of tips and tricks you can add to your arsenal as you begin taking responsibility for your emotions and seeking to manage your anger properly. Let's start with what you can do in the moment when your anger flares up.

The breathing exercises I described earlier are a great way to bring yourself down from the precipice of anger. Other options include:

- Engage in a time-out for yourself.
- Drink water to rehydrate.
- Focus on the behaviors you've experienced, not on the person who exhibited them.
- Avoid the use of "why" and "you."
- Avoid the use of rigid words, such as "should," "could," "must," "have to," "never," and "always." This applies both to talking about yourself (e.g. "I should never...") and talking about others (e.g. "You should never...").
- Use grounding exercises, such as rubbing your palms together or touching various objects around you.
- Hum or sing a tune as a distraction to refocus your mind.
- Clean. (This is my favorite because it gives you something to do other than stewing in your anger and can help you to think through the problem.)

There are also several preventative actions you can take over the long-term:

- "Pray without ceasing," as we're instructed in 1 Thessalonians 5:17 (NKJV).
- Meditate on God's Word (Joshua 1:8; Psalm 1:2; Philippians 4:8).
- Speak Scripture out loud.
- Practice self-care, such as eating well, exercising, managing stress, setting boundaries, and getting ample sleep.
- Drink plenty of water.
- Develop a formal time-out so that when an anger event occurs, you can tell others what you're doing and why when you remove yourself from a situation. This kind of explanation is helpful and healthy, especially when it comes to letting a loved one know in what circumstances you'll have to step away for a moment so you can recover. Walking away without so much as a word only lets the problem fester.
- Practice conflict resolution skills, such as acknowledging behaviors and using assertive communication.
- Journal about anger-provoking situations so that you can increase your awareness of triggers, negative self-talk, and poor coping skills as well as

encourage yourself by documenting strengths and areas in which you're showing improvement. I find it helpful to consider two Bible verses here: Proverbs 3:3, which says, "Let love and faithfulness never leave you; bind them around your neck, write them on the tablet of your heart" (NIV); and Habakkuk 2:2, in which God says, "Write down the revelation and make it plain on tablets so that a herald may run with it" (NIV).

- Read or listen to material related to anger management and healthy coping skills.
- Take a walk in nature.
- Practice progressive muscle relaxation by tensing and releasing muscles in a specific manner from toes to head or head to toes. This stress-relieving technique for the body can help to lower blood pressure, anxiety, and depression and promote better sleep.

In addition, I highly recommend implementing the acronym I've developed called REST, which stands for:

- **R**eview the facts.
- **E**dit the false.
- **S**urrender the fear.
- **T**rust the Father.

I developed the REST process when I was working with a client to eliminate overthinking on her part. First, **review** the facts to make sure that the narrative in your head is accurate. Are the things you say to yourself aligning with what God's Word tells you? This is where Satan loves to attack us, so in that review, identify the false statements. Then **edit** those statements, removing the parts that are lies from the enemy. Once you've done that, **surrender** your fear, whatever it happens to be in that situation, and **trust** in what the Father says through His Word that He will do.

You don't need to succumb to the lies you're told about anger. Through the mindsets and practical actions we've discussed, you can develop healthy management of your anger so that this emotion will release its grip on your life.

Burt's sermon: The reward—the point is that I stayed w Jesus

WORKBOOK

Chapter Five Questions

Question: In what circumstances, at what times of day, and with what people do you tend to feel angry?

"Church" people.
I need my ladies small group but I also feel frustrated a lot.

I appreciated Ellen apologizing. She truth @ Annapolis EP w that I was already w/ to w/ the fellowship, visitors, and the fact that Marc is so attached there confirms extinction.

Question: What may be the primary emotion motivating your anger? How can you begin taking responsibility for your emotions?

Fear is primary - Fear that I won't have what I need. Like when I "ran away" at age 16 - To White Lake - w/ $14.00 in my pocket. I needed to get to some peace + quiet out of the drama + trauma that was my "home." ★ I didn't have what I needed to do that safely. Now I do + I can rely on God + the path he's shown the LLC

Question: Of the practical measures described in this chapter for managing your anger, which ones will you begin employing this week?

_____
_____
_____
_____
_____
_____

Action: Choose one situation in which you regularly experience anger and apply the REST process to it. *Review* the narrative in your head regarding why you are angry and *edit* the parts that don't align with what God's Word says about you, your emotions, and other people. Then *surrender* your emotions to your heavenly Father and choose to *trust* in Him.

Primary emotions: → Drill ★
Fear — p. 106
Shame

Build strategies to make me feel safe.
Notice — my physical reactions
Then the aggression toward other people.
★ Be realistic in expectations

Chapter Six Notes

☆ Underneath my anger toward Marc is fear that God won't provide + take care of us.

I've been treating myself the way I've been treating my flooring downstairs — abrasive + doing damage. Help me restore my own luster, texture + "shine."

11/22/2023 — That like when I was 16 + ran away I will again be vulnerable + alone in danger. No!

☆ The truth is I have a good Father, who does and is caring + providing well for me. And he loves, enjoys, takes great pride in caring + providing for me.

Prov- "I can" laugh without fear of
31:25 the future." He is good, I am strong in him, I am able by the equipping of the master. He and I are on a wonderful journey together, on a beautiful adventure + I will praise him.

CHAPTER SEVEN

Our Inner Child and Attachment Style

Whatever our valley of dry bones looks like, being stuck there has a lot to do with lack of connection. It could be a feeling of disconnection that drags us into that desolate place, or it could be our depressed or anxious thoughts that pull us there, leading us to isolate.

When and where do we develop these complex, roiling emotions? More importantly, how did we learn the ways we deal with them, whether healthy or unhealthy? As with most other aspects of our lives, it all began when we were kids. No matter how much we grow up, that training remains a part of us. You may have a steady job, a car, and a marriage, and you may pay your taxes on time. But inside, you may still be a kid wrestling with the good and the bad of your upbringing.

We all have an inner child. This is the part of us that's fun, spontaneous, and curious. Who doesn't want that to be the part of themselves that receives the most attention and has the most influence over their personality? When we're connected to our inner child in a healthy manner, we're full of wonder, inspiration, and excitement. This aspect of our mental self has a profound influence on our overall personality, and being disconnected from it due to emotional wounds means that we tend to be negative, depressed, and mistrustful. Anxiety and depression are more likely to rear their heads.

The famed psychologist Carl Jung first proposed the concept of the inner child. He suggested that this part of us is a prime influence on every decision we make. The inner child hasn't grown up, and it stores all the memories and emotions that came with our earliest experiences. It stockpiles the joy we gained from happy events but also absorbs the negative things that happened to us, including the wounds inflicted by the people who were supposed to keep us safe.

When we are hurt as children, those wounds impact how we think, behave, and relate to others, even after we become adults. The inner child absorbs and holds on to negative emotions triggered by caregivers, who were supposed to keep us safe. If our needs were not met, our sense of safety is either riddled with gaping holes like a worn-out net or was completely ripped apart and is now useless. This makes us hypervigilant, looking for threats around every corner and in every shadow. We believe that the world is inherently unsafe and so live in a constant state of fear, at least inwardly.

That fear is most often rooted in abandonment. Tim Clinton and Gary Sibcy wrote in *Why You Do the Things You Do*, "Thankfully, God programmed us to know from birth that when our caregivers are not nearby, danger lurks. This truth supports a crucial point in our discussion: fear of abandonment is the fundamental human fear. It is so basic and so profound that it emerges even before we acquire the language to voice it."[15]

Those terrified inner children don't disappear. The adults who harbor them have unknowingly found ways to suppress that fear.

How Children Connect

I used to work with children in a clinical setting, but after a while, it became clear that in order to help them the most, I needed to reparent their parents. Why? Often the issues the children were dealing with were products of their parents' upbringing and how they reacted to negative behavior.

Children tend to be products of their environment and the nurturing they receive from caregivers. If parents or other caregivers have insecure attachment styles, they really don't understand the impact they have on their children. Most times, they will benefit from learning new skills so they don't respond to negative behavior in an inappropriate or counterproductive manner. Working with parents to provide clarity for the reasons behind inappropriate behaviors, foster an environment of healthy change, and practice improved coping skills ultimately benefits the children as well.

Often parents would expect their child to "get better" miraculously through the therapy he or she received, but they didn't want to do anything different at home. Some parents would still dismiss or disapprove of their child's feelings.

They might ignore those feelings, use sarcasm to criticize them, or even punish them. Those parents don't want to change, because it's hard for them to see their own struggles and acknowledge their own childhood wounds.

That's why I switched my focus to adults. I wanted to help them dig back into their own childhoods so we could look at how they were raised and, from there, see if we could provide an improved environment for their children.

It all has to do with our *attachment styles*, the ways we bonded with our caregivers when they raised us. We all have stories about our childhoods. Some are glowing, happy memories, and others still elicit strong fears or anxieties. The latter type has a tremendous impact on how we react emotionally to people and situations.

Types of Attachment Styles

When discussing attachment styles, I lean on the models derived from John Bowlby's work by Mary Ainsworth and others. There are four attachment types that encompass most people's behavior.

Secure

These individuals were raised to feel safe, seen, known, and valued. Throughout childhood, their caregivers comforted and reassured them in times of emotional distress while simultaneously encouraging them to understand their emotions. Self-soothing was included in this emotional training.

The caregivers of these children were constant, predictable presences, and they were aware of their own emotional health. Rather than leaning on their children to manage their personal insecurities, these caregivers explored other resources that served as healthier outlets.

Children raised in the secure attachment style grow up to be comfortable expressing their emotions. They base their relationships on honesty and emotional closeness, but they don't depend on a partner's approval and tend to have a positive view of themselves. These adults usually relate to others authentically and honestly because they have an internal sense of security that was instilled in them as children.

Avoidant/Dismissive

Individuals raised in this style are referred to as *anxious/avoidant*. Their caregivers didn't tolerate emotional expression, in part because they themselves were emotionally distant. They expected their children to be independent.

As adults, avoidant/dismissive individuals tend to avoid emotional closeness, but that doesn't necessarily mean that they're entertaining an overwhelming number of negative thoughts. They may feel that they don't need to be in a relationship to be complete since they have a positive view of themselves. These adults also tend to suppress feelings when in an emotionally tense situation.

Anxious/Preoccupied

People raised this way are referred to as *anxious/ambivalent*. *Inconsistency* is the key word to remember here. Their caregivers met their needs at some times and not at others, without apparent rhyme or reason. Security was never guaranteed.

Those caregivers might have sought closeness with their children to satisfy their own emotional needs rather than focusing on the children's needs. They might have been seen as overprotective or intrusive, but those behaviors were actually undertaken for their own benefit.

When these children become adults, they often have a strong fear of abandonment. For them, getting attention from a partner is the cure for anxiety. They need approval, and without it, they tend to become needy, demanding, and desperate for love. They have low self-esteem and are insecure. They never think that they're good enough but tend to think very highly of others.

They may also be jealous and suspicious and tend to have an external locus of control. People with an external locus of control generally hold the belief that they have no control over circumstances. Their reactions tend to depend on what's going on around them or within their relationships. When things don't go their way, they're prone to thinking, "Why bother trying?" Do you remember Eeyore, the gloomy donkey in the Winnie-the-Pooh books by A. A. Milne? We may think of a pessimistic person with a lack of confidence and limited agency as someone with "Eeyore syndrome."

Disorganized/Fearful-Avoidant

This attachment style shows what happens when the people who should be providing support wind up doing the exact opposite. For children who grew up this way, their caregivers produced fear in them. The caregivers were emotionally unavailable and unresponsive when the children sought attention, support, and affection. They might have taken it a terrible step further and inflicted abuse.

As adults, these individuals are torn. They want to be emotionally intimate but have deep-seated fears about trusting and depending on others. They have poor emotional regulation and tend to avoid relationships for fear of getting hurt. They may be just as inconsistent in their behaviors as their caregivers were and may find themselves struggling with substance abuse or mental-health issues. It's one of the most difficult attachment styles to overcome.

Clinton and Sibcy touched on these more difficult upbringings, explaining, "People with an insecure relationship style (ambivalent, avoidant, or disorganized) tend to question their self-worth, and they don't expect their caregivers to be there for them. Insecure styles can make people hypersensitive to soul injuries. In fact, some people with certain insecure styles almost expect to be betrayed and abandoned because, in the past, their support figures have repeatedly let them down."[16]

My dear friend Leslie T. Dean wrote in her book, *Forgiven Much*, "There is a place deep inside every little girl's heart to be loved and protected. ... When those things are absent she develops a void."[17]

CONNECTING WITH THE INNER CHILD

So, how can it benefit you to know where you fit into these attachment styles? Understanding your emotional functioning is key to navigating life successfully. Your attachment style impacts every aspect of your life, including your mental health. Knowing these styles helps you to gain insight into how you developed as a child based on the way you were parented.

It can be a difficult chain of events to assemble. If, for example, my grandparents parented my parents in a dismissive way, they might have done so based on what they knew and how they were raised. They passed along those upbringing methods to my parents, who passed them on to me, and then I passed them on to my children. This is the passing of the land of dry bones from parents to children for generations.

Scripture makes reference to "visiting the iniquity of the fathers upon the children and the children's children to the third and the fourth generation" (Exodus 34:7 NKJV), and, in a way, I see that in the transmission of attachment styles. We often accept the unacceptable. We find ourselves becoming comfortable with the uncomfortableness of unhealthy parenting. I think that, a lot of times, kids think that what they're experiencing is normal. They tell themselves, "That's how everybody's parents are."

Our families, beginning generations ago, set up their

camps in the valley of dry bones by inadvertently fostering unhealthy parenting models. We don't consider finding a way out, because we think that's where we're supposed to be, until someone comes along and cries out, "No, it's not okay! There's a better way to do this!"

It's important to keep in mind that we shouldn't look at these parts of our upbringing to find fault or cast blame. It's more helpful if we look into our childhoods to try to connect the dots for the purpose of clarifying any emotional limits we may have with ourselves and in our relationships and identifying the patterns in our emotional behaviors. We're looking for clues into the areas where we need the most change in order to improve our relationships.

The Empty Chair

How do you facilitate this conversation with the inner child? I'm a fan of the Gestalt empty chair technique. Gestalt therapy was originally founded by Fritz and Laura Perls in 1940 as a form of person-centered psychotherapy that focuses on personal responsibility and staying in the present and is used to increase a person's awareness, direction, and freedoms. The empty chair technique is role-play designed to allow an individual to express thoughts and feelings in a safe environment. Even if you aren't familiar with Gestalt therapy, you may have heard of the empty chair technique in the context of working through interpersonal conflict or grief. This method involves sitting across from an empty chair and imagining someone or some aspect of yourself in that chair.

What would you say to that person or that part of yourself?

If it were me in need of help, I would look at that empty seat and imagine the little-girl version of me. She could be whatever age would be most helpful to me for the process, perhaps three or four years old, with blonde hair and blue eyes, swinging her legs because the chair's too big for her. I can see her there. I'm watching her, and she's watching me. What would I have wanted that little girl to hear from her parents when she was going through the situations that I know had a negative impact?

I've found this to be a powerful technique because it connects different aspects of our personalities. That little girl might have been stuck in an emotional corner after dealing with adults, telling herself, "No, don't say anything. Don't talk. You'll just get in trouble. What happens in this house stays in this house." Her parents might have been the kind to dismiss or even ridicule her emotions. With the empty chair technique, that child has the chance to be seen and heard. I can acknowledge this facet of who I am and talk about the negative things I experienced.

What would you say to a four-year-old who is getting fussy or having trouble focusing? You would ask, "Are you hungry?" or "Are you tired?" You would explore the problem and try to find a solution, not lash out and say, "You're dumb," or "You're lazy," as we tend to tell our adult selves.

The empty chair technique gives us the chance to hug that inner child and say, "You know what, you're doing what you do because that's what you know how to do. There's nothing wrong with you. We're just learning how to do it differently."

Finding the Bones

Years ago, my husband and I wanted to buy a piece of property that was next door to us. We didn't have anything outrageous in mind. The plan was to tear it down and build an office in its place.

To call the property depressed was to put it mildly. The house was more than just run-down; it was full of garbage. Heaps of junk littered the lawn and filled the house. Whoever had lived there before hadn't bothered to get rid of any of it. There was a boatload of debris, and when I say boatload, I mean there was an actual boat on the property that was full of trash and also hiding more piles of trash behind it.

We removed nine construction dumpsters' worth of garbage from that property before we could even begin to see beneath what was covering the surface. The experience of cleaning it all out did not make me love the place more. In fact, I was more than ready to tear everything down and start over from a flattened lot, but the contractor we brought in disagreed. "Look," he said, "you don't want to tear this whole house down. It has good bones."

He meant that although the property had been left to rot and the exterior had so many problems that it was overwhelming even to begin thinking about how to address them, the core of the home was well-built and strong. The house had a good foundation. And so do I.

We took this contractor's advice to heart and began the long, difficult process of restoration, which included stripping the house down to its bones. During that process, an older gentleman, who might have been in his nineties, stopped by with his adult children. It turned out that he had lived in the farmhouse years ago and wanted to see what was going on. He was in tears because he had seen the place he'd called home lapse into terrible disrepair and was now witnessing its rebirth. His distress overwhelmed him, but the way he described how the house had first been built really stuck with me.

This gentleman told us that the wooden beams had come from trees on the farmland that had been knocked down by a rough storm. Those good bones our contractor had praised weren't picked up at the local hardware store; they had been hewn from battle-scarred logs.

I thought it was appropriate that storms had created that house. So often, we find ourselves with generational struggles, like family scars that have been passed down from grandparent to parent to child, and we feel like there's nothing worthwhile left because of all the damage. We see only the mounds of trash piled up from decades of unhealthy emotional responses and warped feelings.

A house like that seems to reflect the emotional turmoil of the people who once inhabited it. Somebody stopped caring about the health and well-being of the property, like we too often stop caring about the health and well-being of a relationship. Then others moved in with their own crap and let it pile up wherever they felt it might work. You may be wondering, "Didn't they know it was junk that did nothing good and only littered the place?" They might not have known. Don't forget that when it comes to unhealthy ways of living, coping, and expressing emotion, those ways may be all someone has ever known.

In reality, there may be strong bones hidden underneath all of the garbage on the surface. When it comes to diving into our pasts and discovering the attachment styles we learned in childhood and have maintained as adults, we're not looking to cast blame. We're hauling away the garbage to find what's underneath: the good, strong bones that will help to carry us through to the next phases of our lives.

You may feel that your bones are dry, but there is someone who can make them strong and full of life again. Your Father in heaven stands ready to reattach sinew and stimulate muscle. I wanted to put a reminder of this truth into the house my husband and I were renovating. In the middle of the long, painful process of restoring the house, I began writing Scripture verses all over the exposed beams, using permanent marker so the words would last.

Today, the house is again a home, with God's Word embedded in its very frame and its original purpose restored. It's now the place where my son and family live. Like this house, we need God's Word embedded in our bones to make them strong and resilient and to fill us with purpose.

Putting It to Use

God said, "My people are destroyed for lack of knowledge" (Hosea 4:6 NKJV). This was meant in a spiritual sense, as in knowledge of God and His ways, but I think that it also applies to knowledge of ourselves in this world. The

Strategies

more we know about our attachment styles and the attachment styles of our loved ones, the better we're able to relate to one another.

Gary Chapman's *The Five Love Languages* puts this concept into concrete terms to which most people can relate.[18] My husband, for example, expresses his love through acts of service while I desire quality time spent together. Knowing how each of us seeks attachment with a loved one helps to synchronize our relationship and guide our expectations.

Knowledge is key, but how do we put that knowledge into practice? How do we, as adults, prevent ourselves from behaving in an immature fashion when we're challenged in emotionally charged situations? Below are some practical steps we can take as we seek to grow in this area:

- Work to challenge and overcome the negative thoughts and self-defeating tendencies in our personality and attachment style. There are aspects of the way we were raised that we don't have to listen to, live by, or pass on to the next generation. *[migrating to emotionally unavailable men]*

- Reinforce our positive aspects. Find the things that are good and helpful and bring those to the surface. *[Build on the positive parts of my foundation: Faith, humor, business sense]*

- Identify our needs. If we don't know what we need, how can we take care of our needs?

- Adjust your expectations of yourself and others. Other people may not think the same way you do *["Hurt people, hurt people."]*

- Avoid neglecting your needs to fulfill someone else's. You've probably heard the saying that "you can't help others unless you help yourself." Well, it's true! Self-care is important if you want to extend a hand to others in need.

  [handwritten: A lifestyle change for me]

- Use assertive communication skills. Be clear about your issues and your needs. Make them known to others around you so you have help available when you need it. Effective communication also helps us to navigate differences so we can let go of unrealistic expectations and create realistic ones, as we'll see in the next chapter.

- Rely on God's power and grace and find your identity and value in His redemption. God tells us that we are His children, and Jesus said, "Let the little children come to me, and do not hinder them" (Luke 18:16 NIV). God's desire is to bring His children back into the fold, no matter their hurts, and offer them His love and forgiveness.

These steps are some of the most powerful ones we can take when we're seeking a way out of the valley of dry bones. It may seem like a long, difficult journey, but if we take the hand of our inner child on one side and Christ's hand on the other, then it won't be nearly as dark and lonely as we first think.

I love the house renovation analogy.

WORKBOOK

Chapter Seven Questions

Question: With which of the four attachment styles do you most identify? What do you now know about how you function emotionally that you didn't understand before?

Anxious-Preoccupied. I was trained to be "used" for the emotional needs of others but main they were ill-equipped or uninterested (dad) = attending, after divorce in Laie + move back to N.C., my dad's response over dinner to Susie+Hep wood - "I don't have time for it." Referring to his outbursts + belittling statements to me earlier that day claiming "I couldn't keep a commitment." He really is a sick individual + I'm grateful to be protected from him + from my mom's manipulation attempts.

Question: What aspects of your personality and attachment style do you need to challenge and overcome? What aspects do you need to draw to the surface and reinforce?

① Challenge — That I'm really not that talented or set apart for special purpose(s). That others are more able and more valuable. Not true. I am the Esther of Caregiving.

② Draw to the surface: Faith, leadership, Humor, and strong business sense and acumen.

Question: What does God say about your inner child?

That he formed me in my mother's womb — I am fearfully + wonderfully made. I am a child, a daughter of the King. I am wealthy!

When I was a toddler I spent time w/ Aunt Sue, Bernice + later Jay, Cat, Frankie, Jerry. I was physically cute + funny. ~~I also had scarlet fever + german measles simultaneously — Very serious. Aunt Sue took me to "The Lion's Den" snack downstairs — the dime store + I dreamed of a life of travel + big adventures. Aunt Bernice is an artist + taught me how to draw a~~

Action: Use the empty chair technique to have a conversation with your inner child. Picture yourself as a kid. What did you need to hear at that age? What needs did you have that were not met? Allow yourself to be vulnerable. This is an opportunity to acknowledge what you experienced and how you felt as a child and to explore how this part of you may be affecting how you live today.

bunch of grapes (correctly). She praised my artistic ability. She also tucked me in + left a banana by the bed in case I woke up hungry — That really made an impression on me of tenderness + thoughtfulness.

"Anxiety" - holds us hostage to the past + the future + robs us of the "present"

Chapter Seven Notes

My dad's behavior made healthy "connection" impossible. I learned to "want" or expect the exact opposite of what I truly needed + wanted emotionally because that seemed to work.

→ As an adult it does NOT work.

★ Help me to reconnect to my inner Wendy.

p.120 - Caregivers were too overwhelmed to take own needs.

★ p.122 ? Can I learn to "parent" well myself + heal these gaps?

1/24/2023 p.126 "Anxious-preoccupied" fits my parenting. I'm not an Eyore-type person but I was "used" as a source of meeting mom's vast emotional needs.

p.128 I would speak to the 1st or 3rd grader who wasn't "cute or petite" enough to be the star of the Christmas play: Denise Moffatt but rather was in the choir. I thought that was why my dad didn't

> *Carry me in arms – so proud of his little girl like Denise Moffatt's dad did. I think he did hold my hand – but clearly I had to stand on my own 2 feet + walk beside him.*

CHAPTER EIGHT

Creating Realistic Expectations

Do you remember the hypothetical man I mentioned in Chapter Three, who was "supposed" to hold the door for me as I entered a business? Of course, he didn't know that, so for whatever reason, he didn't. Maybe he was raised differently from how I was. Maybe he was raised to hold open the door for the next person, but he was having a rough day or was distracted and didn't realize that he wasn't extending the courtesy.

The important part of this hypothetical scenario is my expectation that this man would hold the door open for me as a matter of good manners. Why did I have this expectation? That's how the men around me were raised, so that behavior was what I expected to encounter. When the man didn't hold open the door, my expectations were shattered, and that shattering provoked a negative emotional response.

Our expectations shape everything about our lives. We formulate how we're going to react based on what we expect to encounter, and when reality proves very different from what we've imagined—which happens a great deal of the time—the outcome can be fraught with difficulty.

NAMING OUR EMOTIONS AND ACKNOWLEDGING OUR FEELINGS

One of my favorite movies of all time is Pixar Animation's *Inside Out*.[19] It has to be one of the best depictions of what emotional control looks like and how the struggle to achieve it plays out.

The main character, Riley, is an eleven-year-old girl from Minnesota who loves hockey. Her emotions steer her through life in dramatic fashion, with each major emotion portrayed by a different actor in anthropomorphized form. These emotions hang out in her head, which is depicted as a fantastical, futuristic control center. Joy takes the lead in most of Riley's experiences, but when the family moves to San Francisco, Sadness takes over more often. The other three emotions—Anger, Disgust, and Fear—start exerting an increasing amount of control.

You can already see where this is going. An inciting event, a life change she can't control, pushes Riley out of her comfort zone. What specifically is it about the family's move to a new state that proves unsettling? It's the way her expectations, however reasonable or unreasonable they may be, go unmet.

Riley's parents change some of the constants in her life:

Creating Realistic Expectations

her home and her friends. They do their best to be loving parents and try to help their daughter adjust by hyping up how great San Francisco is. However, Riley internalizes that hype and builds exaggerated expectations around it because she has no other frame of reference.

You can see the result in one of the first scenes, when Riley arrives in San Francisco with her parents. She sees the iconic Golden Gate Bridge dominating the skyline. One would think that a child from Minnesota would be impressed with something so architecturally awe-inspiring, but her emotion Joy comments, "Hey, look! The Golden Gate Bridge! Isn't that great? It's not made out of solid gold like we thought, which is kind of a disappointment, but still!"

This response tells me that Riley's expectations are based on the hype that has built her frame of reference. Her parents have probably talked to her about the bridge, given how excited they are about the trip to a new city, but she processes it through her eleven-year-old frame of reference. When reality doesn't meet her expectations, Riley's Joy attempts to minimize that disappointment rather than naming the emotion and tackling it head-on. It turns out to be the first of many disappointments Riley experiences, and Joy can't keep up with them, no matter how she tries to minimize their impact.

I highly recommend this film, not only for how it emphasizes the importance of naming our emotions and acknowledging feelings like sadness, but also for the seriousness with which it treats things like emotional impact on memories.

DINNER TIME!

Expectations are tied to our values, our beliefs, our needs, and our desires. Like most things, we acquire them in childhood. Our families teach us what to expect in life, and these expectations cover everything from the condition of wealth or poverty in which we will live to how other people will treat us.

When our expectations are realistic, they help us to explore, dream about, and excel in our values and desires. They keep us striving for better results and to be better people.

When our expectations are unrealistic, they keep us mired in the "shoulds"—as in, what we and other people *should* do, feel, and think. Just like I did with the man who didn't hold the door, we sabotage ourselves and our interactions with other people when we think in terms of what *should* be. We end up feeling guilty and torturing ourselves over why things don't happen the way we think they should. This is a recipe for increased anxiety and depression.

The problem is that "shoulds" don't reflect what's actually happening. It's like the fight-or-flight instinct I addressed when discussing anxiety earlier in this book. We're focused on something that isn't actually happening and may never take place. We end up stuck in the mentality that we and others are not living up to the expectations we set in place. Resentment and bitterness take hold when other people don't do what we think they should do.

We form expectations about the most trivial things, and they hold fast throughout our lives. For example, I came from a small family, and my father determined that dinner should be on the table and ready to eat by a certain time, usually when he got home from work. His expectations dictated not only when we were all going to eat, but also what was on the menu. He wanted meat, potatoes, and a vegetable, followed by dessert (naturally). This is what he expected of my mother every weeknight, and she met those expectations without fail.

That was normal for me, and I assumed that I was expected to do the same for my husband when I got married. As a newlywed, I decided that I was going to recreate what had served, in my family, as the proper way to eat dinner.

There was difficulty in copying this tradition from the get-go because my husband's work was not nearly as predictable as my father's had been, but that didn't deter me. I vowed to get around the irregular dinner hour and focus on the meal itself.

One night, I went for it big time: steak Diane, garlic mashed potatoes, fresh vegetables, and a dessert, all made well in advance from scratch. Talk about setting the bar high for myself! The sheer time spent was overwhelming, and since we had a tiny kitchen, the cramped space added to the difficulty. But I got it done and had it ready at a reasonable hour. I was sure that my parents would have been proud.

My husband came home from work to a house full of wonderful smells. I must have been beaming and probably just a little pleased with myself. I plated his food and handed it to him, ready to hear glowing compliments about how great the meal was.

What did my husband do? He took the plate, turned right

around to the refrigerator, and grabbed a piece of baloney. He slapped it on his plate and then followed up that alteration to the night's entrée with a dollop of mayonnaise.

I couldn't believe it! If you've seen any of the cartoons in which the character gets so mad that there's steam coming out of its ears, then you have a sense of what I felt in that moment. Talk about expectations being subverted!

What was wrong with my husband? Was it that he didn't appreciate the food? He assured me that wasn't the case. He simply wanted baloney and mayo as a side dish.

That answer didn't placate me. How could he possibly want something else, something more, after the feast I'd set before him? I spent all that time and energy sweating in the kitchen, only to have my husband put a slice of cold cuts on his plate right next to a meal that should have been on the cover of a cooking magazine!

It turned out that I had been so focused on my expectations, which had been formulated by my family experience, that I had completely discounted my husband's experience and expectations. My husband came from a huge family, and in that household, people ate whenever they were ready to eat. Dinnertime wasn't so much a single set time as it was a window of opportunity. The quality of food also wasn't something he worried about. There was no need to fawn over a meal prepared by a diligent cook. For his family, constrained as they were by time and budget, it was less about what and when they ate than about eating at all.

That moment was an eye-opening experience that forced us to take a hard look at our expectations and bring them into sync, especially on my part. For instance, it didn't take me long to adjust my cooking style. Even though I didn't give up being a cook—and am still a pretty good one, if I do say so myself—I didn't make things harder on myself than necessary.

For his part, my husband also learned to develop new expectations about food in our married life. One of the first meals I made him was a one-pot dish. He bounced into the house, excited because of the amazing smell of food coming from our kitchen. He opened the lid eagerly but then said, with disappointment, "Oh. This looks like someone already ate it."

He reluctantly tried it anyway and then couldn't stop bragging about how good it was. He vowed never again to judge food based on what it looked like, and from then on, he has been open to eating everything I have made.

DRY BONES TERRITORY

Refusal to adjust or even acknowledge our expectations can lead us into the valley of dry bones. This is especially true when "should" comes into play. When we focus on what isn't instead of what is, we stay stuck in negative emotions. There we go again, setting up camp in the desolate wasteland that the Lord would much rather we steered clear of. On the other hand, shifting our focus to what is, with gratitude, helps us to manage our expectations in a healthy way.

Denying what is has a way of distorting our thinking, and we believe that things are happening to us or because of us.

It's another example of the blame game that we learn at an early age, except in this case, we're more than willing to share the blame when the "should" statements start invading our minds.

If we believe that other people are causing our misery, we may think that they should do something different. Those people, of course, don't change their behavior. Why should they? In most cases, they're acting in response to their own expectations and have no idea what we think they should do and why. That doesn't stop us from reacting emotionally. We see ourselves as entitled to other people's consideration, and when they don't change, emotions such as disappointment and anger kick in.

In this case, *entitlement* is the belief that we deserve more from a person or situation than what we are receiving. We begin hostile inner talk, such as "Who do they think they are?" We continue to interpret events through this lens, aggressively reinforcing our belief that we deserve more, until we're firmly established in a mentality of entitlement.

To look at it from another angle, if we believe that we're at fault, then we begin the process of self-deprecation, which may result in anxiety and depression. The hostile self-talk is inwardly directed: "Who do I think I am?" We may believe that we don't deserve better than what we're experiencing, which is dangerous because it can lead not only to an increase in anxious thoughts, but also to the slippery slope into depression. This way of interpreting events and interactions reinforces our belief that we're not as assertive in getting our needs met as we should be.

Either one of these reactions can be self-sabotaging because they set up ourselves and others for failure. It's unrealistic to believe that we deserve or are entitled to have everything go our way all of the time. That's simply not how the world works. It's equally unrealistic to believe that we don't deserve for anything ever to go our way. In Chapter Three, we saw how both mindsets played out in the example of getting pulled over by the police for speeding.

- Some other examples of unrealistic expectations I've heard are:
- "My wife should know how I am feeling without me telling her."
- "My children should be grateful for all I do for them."
- "I should get that job because I'm the best person for the job."
- "I should be perfect."
- "I should have known better than to ask someone for help."

Unrealistic expectations assume a level of control that we don't have over a person or situation, and they set us up for repeated disappointments. Sometimes things are simply out of our hands, no matter what we do to convince ourselves otherwise. The facts are the facts, and trying to frame the narrative in a different way isn't always helpful.

RIDING OUT MY EXPECTATIONS

My amazing friend Donna and I used to ride bikes several times a week. We would ride, on average, fifteen miles each time, which we thought was a respectable distance, so we decided to start entering bike rides for charitable events.

The distances in those events were much farther. Donna and I took part in 35-, 50-, and 75-mile rides with success. That 75-mile trip was a long, hard day, and we finished among the last of the riders, but we finished!

At the end of that ride, I realized that my back wheel's brake had been stuck in place, which made pedaling more difficult than it should have been. Instead of being upset or frustrated, I was even prouder of how I'd ridden since I had no idea when that brake had gotten stuck. It could have slowed me down the entire 75 miles for all I knew! Based on that experience, I expected the next ride to be a cinch. History, after all, is a predictor of the future, right?

Donna and I signed up for a shorter, thirty-five-mile ride, and I made sure that my bike was fully functional. I should point out that we weren't riding the fancy, slim-wheeled models you might see winding through the hilly routes of the Tour de France. No, these were your average thick-wheeled three-speeds from Walmart.

This 35-mile ride was in April. It began in a beach town and wove inland before putting us back at the starting point. The day was windy, so going inland helped because trees and buildings offered some protection. The last five miles of the ride was a stretch of highway between beach towns, with the ocean on the right and the bay on the left, which meant that it was much more exposed to the wind.

Once Donna and I turned onto the highway and headed for the finish line, the wind really picked up. Donna is older than I am but in much better shape, so she takes the lead and sets the pace. I was struggling to keep going. If I had gotten off and walked the bike, I would probably have gone faster. I noticed young children who were riding with their families passing me with no problem. I couldn't wrap my head around how difficult it was for me to keep my bike moving forward, so I assumed that silly brake must have been stuck again.

Donna was getting ahead of me until she realized how far behind I was. Then she periodically stopped and waited for me to catch up. "Bless her heart," as the saying goes. Finally, I yelled at her, "Girl, this is not 'no man left behind'! This is 'save yourself'! Keep going and get to the finish line!" I wanted her to complete the race and not have to wait on me. I also thought that if she did get to the finish, she could load her bike into the car and come rescue me from the last five miles of this never-ending ride!

I managed to finish without being rescued, but make no mistake, it was a brutal slog. One of the first things I did after getting off that bike was to check the brake—and no, it wasn't stuck. I couldn't blame my difficulty on a malfunction, but I had expected to do so much better on that 35-mile ride than I did. After all, I felt like I had done better on a ride that was over twice as long, with a stuck brake.

I had set my expectations based on one experience and allowed them to dictate how I should feel during another event. That 35-mile ride was more difficult for me than the 75-mile ride. Perhaps more importantly, the whole experience had nothing to do with the ride and everything to do with the rider. My brake wasn't stuck. It was windy, but there were hundreds of other people participating, so it wasn't like a hurricane posed a threat. There were no excuses I could fall back on. Now Donna and I spend our time sitting at the beach instead.

CASTING ASIDE UNREALISTIC EXPECTATIONS

Holding on to unrealistic expectations can lead to humorous moments like the one I just shared, but more often it's harmful. Consider if you have the expectation that you somehow deserve certain kinds of individuals in your relationships, even if you know that their unhealthy habits will be bad for you, too. Sticking with your expectation of deserving relationships with only these types of people can negatively impact your mental and physical health and lead you into unsafe situations.

There was a man who might be the most infamous example of how holding on to unrealistic expectations leads to a bad end. That man's name was Judas Iscariot.

On a simple level, Judas expected something that wasn't going to happen: the overthrow of the Roman occupiers and the restoration of a king to the throne of Israel. Judas wanted Jesus to be that guy, even though Jesus preached that His kingdom was not a kingdom of the world.

What about the deeper, hidden expectations that Judas might have harbored? I've always suspected that Judas had a very definite idea of how much money he was owed—for what reasons, we may never know. Scripture is clear that Judas took money from the common purse the disciples used (John 12:6). Since he was the manager of the money, this was fairly easy to do. He's one of the most ancient recorded examples of an embezzler.

Did the disciples know about this, or did they find out later? John didn't spell that out in his Gospel. I find the situation interesting because Jesus chose Judas, knowing all along that Judas would betray Him. There was Judas, walking with Jesus, witnessing the miracles being performed, and seeing people being freed from physical ailments and even death. All the while, he was stealing from the money bag. He even had the nerve to complain about how much the woman who anointed Jesus' feet with oil had wasted (John 12:5). It sure sounds like Judas's greed talking in that story, even though he asserted that the money should have been used for the poor instead.

Judas had clear expectations of what bringing the kingdom of heaven to earth meant, but they were unrealistic. They weren't even close to what Jesus was proclaiming. Jesus wasn't fulfilling Judas's expectations, and because Judas was narrow-minded, he couldn't see the big picture. He didn't assess and reevaluate his expectations based on what Jesus was actually teaching to determine if they were realistic. Instead, he decided to take action. If Jesus wasn't going to fulfill Judas's expectations, then He had to get out of the way for someone else who would.

Not until Judas had been given the thirty pieces of silver did the enormity of what he had done strike him. He flung the money back at the priests and begged for a second chance, but they were all too happy to take the money back and keep Jesus in custody (Matthew 27:3–6). Judas wanted a do-over, but it was too late. That led to the darkest of Judas's expectations, one that ended in his death by his own hand: he expected to be punished. He expected a penalty for how he had betrayed Jesus.

Let's pause here for a moment and speak to the thoughts that tell us that taking our own lives is an option. We see how difficult it would have been for Judas to know Jesus' forgiveness, but it was available to him. Suicide is never the answer. We have the rest of the story in Jesus. If you or someone you know is having suicidal thoughts or urges, please reach out for help. Call a friend or the Suicide and Crisis Lifeline at 988. Go to the emergency room. There's nothing you have done that would make suicide the right or only option for your life. You are too important, valuable, and loved.

Judas knew of Jesus, but he didn't know Jesus. If he had, he would have expected Jesus to offer him forgiveness for what he had done. The unwillingness to reexamine his expectations led Judas so far down into the valley of dry bones that he didn't only pitch his tent there, but brought his life to a close, even as Christ stood ready to breathe new life into his bones.

CREATING REALISTIC EXPECTATIONS

Unrealistic expectations tend to be rigid, with no room for flexibility. At times, we use hindsight to find blame or fault, which isn't helpful because it continues the cycle of self-defeat. It's hard to let go of unrealistic expectations, and we may even use them as a protective measure, because letting them go or adjusting them may set us up for fear. Fear of what? Of being taken advantage of in some manner.

There's a whole slew of ways in which this manifests, and it brings us back to the problem of the "shoulds." You may tell yourself, "I shouldn't tell my spouse how I feel, because she'll use it against me," or "I should ask for help, but if I do, I'll feel weak."

I often point my clients to ways around these types of thoughts after introducing them to anger and anxiety education and the Rational Emotive Behavioral Therapy (REBT) model of challenging their thoughts. My goal is to increase their awareness of "should" statements. When they say "should," "would," "could," "have to," "must," "always," or "never," I point it out by modeling how to challenge those thoughts. Many clients have limited awareness of "shoulding" themselves, so I instruct them to write down their "should" statements every time they hear themselves using the word. They come back surprised by how many times they said "should," and you may be surprised by how often you use it as well!

AWARENESS IS KEY

One of the best ways to move past unrealistic expectations and adopt realistic ones is not to avoid them, but to reflect on them. I like to use the double-standard technique, in which the client and I explore what the client's response would be to someone else saying the same thing or holding the same belief that he or she does.

For example, we might examine the statement: "I'm not worth a healthy relationship." What would you say if you heard that sentence coming out of the mouth of one of your friends? You would probably tell your friend, "No, that's not true. You're undervaluing yourself. There are *tons* of reasons why you *are* worth it. Here are a few...."

Our responses tend to become much more rational, measured, and compassionate when we're reacting to a friend's pain rather than our own. If we are going to take the path that leads out of the valley of dry bones, we must receive the same compassion, this time from ourselves.

LOVING WITH ALL OF OUR HEARTS

There are no greater Scripture verses to meditate on than Christ's command in the Gospel of Mark, which He gave in response to a question with which a teacher of the law was trying to trip Him up. This man asked Jesus, "Of all the commandments, which is the most important?" (Mark 12:28 NIV).

Jesus replied, "The most important one ... is this: 'Hear, O Israel: The Lord our God, the Lord is one. Love the Lord your God with all your heart and with all your soul and with all your mind and with all your strength'" (Mark 12:29–30 NIV). Jesus recognized the interconnectedness of body and mind that is key to our well-being.

Jesus didn't stop there. He added, "The second is this: 'Love your neighbor as yourself.' There is no commandment greater than these" (Mark 12:31 NIV).

There's no way we can fulfill Christ's command to cherish and care for our family, our friends, and the community around us if we don't first love ourselves, and that requires identifying and challenging our unrealistic expectations with compassion and truth.

WORKBOOK

Chapter Eight Questions

Question: Think of a moment in your life when you had an expectation subverted. How did you react?

① Negative - Marc, I never expected the depth of need and volatility that I experienced over the 13 years I lived with him. At first I thought it was me - "gaslighting." Then I reached out to counselors + 2016 I spent the summer in Lewes + within 24-36 hours began to heal, feel like myself & put myself back together. I told him I would never let myself get in that condition again.

★ Rita told him "she was in pretty

bad shape." #2) Caregiving I thought would just be a good second job. Once I saw the opportunity I've embraced it & I'm running with it.

Question: In that situation, was your expectation realistic? Why or why not?

Based on what he "presented" yes, but now I know how much he lied & covered up. Also I would have needed to be a professional therapist to "see" the truth.

I'm not sure I expected him to respond to our separation like he has - He is cold. He is so needy & in such pain that he can only "hurt" me. "Hurt people, hurt people."

Question: How can you begin loving your neighbor by setting realistic expectations?

Realistic expectations keep us from setting others up for failure.

★ Realistic expectations of myself will keep me emotionally balanced and calm & peaceful - more joyful.

_____

_____

_____

_____

Action: Increase your awareness of your use of "should" statements, those you speak out loud and those you say to yourself, by making a note every time you use the word *should* over the course of one week. Are you surprised by how often you say "should"? Challenge each "should" statement you made by evaluating whether or not it's based on realistic expectations. Begin transitioning your focus from what-ifs to what is.

I need to break the habit of looking back & thinking I "should" have been things that would have required a therapist lvl of expericence

*★ I was so focused on making sure that I wasn't the same person who hurt Love so deeply that I was unaware of the danger I was in_*

Chapter Eight Notes

p140 My expectations @ the move to D.C. - Mr. Riley "I think D.C. would be an exciting place to live."

Thanksgiving weekend - Great visit w/ Geoff but the loneliness is overwhelming when guests are gone.

P. 141 - Naming it - "I'm exhausted from trying to keep busy to stay joyful + that part of my life being built around work now - makes me feel sad + weary." I need help.

CHAPTER NINE

The Lazarus Marriage

Our emotional states have a tremendous impact on our relationships, and there's no relationship more vital or closer than marriage. It's the joining of two lives to form one, which makes it all the more important that the people involved be open and clear about their expectations and emotional needs.

There are times when a marriage wanders into the valley of dry bones, whether through intentional neglect or unintentional apathy on the part of one or both spouses. The relationship can become lost there and wither away, just like an individual person. In that case, the work that needs to be done to salvage the bond is intense, because the marriage is in danger of dying. *I think it was dead in 2016.*

Christ is the heavenly expert on finding what is lost and restoring what has died, as He did with His friend Lazarus. After Lazarus died, Jesus took His disciples with Him to visit the tomb. It was a solemn scene, and Jesus expressed His grief through weeping (John 11:35). Tears are perfectly normal when we experience the death of a loved one, and we can also feel a sense of loss and grief when a marriage is fading and withering away. The loss of a dream expectation

But Jesus had a plan (John 11:4, 41–45). He would show the people that God has power over more than lame bodies, unseeing eyes, and tormenting spirits. He can reverse death itself.

That story is why a marriage in need of restoration is called a Lazarus marriage. I first heard the term more than twenty years ago from a pastor's wife who used it to describe the state in which her marriage had been. It was a sobering reminder that even the people whom we consider to be the most holy and the most right with God face the same challenges as all other believers. This woman was giving testimony of how her marriage had been, in her words, "dead and buried." Nothing could breathe life back into it. It was done.

But God performs miracles. He does what cannot be done, as when He brought Lazarus back to life. Nothing is too far gone for Him to bring it back. This woman's marriage wasn't too broken and lifeless for Him to heal it. It was just as God promised Ezekiel. He breathed new life into the dry, dead bones of the marriage. He reattached the tendons and muscles of commitment and love until the marriage could walk around again as if it had never died. Nothing is irretrievable or irreversible for God.

RAISING A MARRIAGE FROM THE DEAD

I wanted to delve more into the idea of a Lazarus marriage but didn't find much that treated the topic of marriage counseling in this way. I had to build up my research from scratch, through my interaction with clients, and I found a lot of things that challenge our understanding about what kills off marriage relationships.

As believers, we need to understand that the enemy plays a significant role in the death of a marriage. He gets into the relationship, sneaking in through the same lies we tell ourselves and listen to when it comes to managing anger and hanging on to unrealistic expectations. He pulls and pushes until the next thing couples know, they are two people wandering separately through the valley of dry bones.

Couples often don't even realize that their marriage is dying. Their relationship becomes fractured. They're disconnected from each other, and each fails to notice the other's fears, worries, and emotions. When they finally do notice a problem and take steps to fix it, whether willingly or unwillingly, the communication is harsh and defensive. I hear a lot of stonewalling, blame-shifting, and gaslighting. The focus shifts to problems with children or troubles at work. Even individual needs can take attention away from the true challenge, which is the restoration of the marriage itself. There's a lot of talking but little listening.

The movie *Fireproof*, starring Kirk Cameron,[20] brings to mind a Lazarus marriage, based on how the characters interact and how their relationship is depicted. The main character, Caleb, is so focused on his job as a fireman and what he sees as his calling, saving people through that job, that he neglects what's far more important in his life: his spouse. She reacts by shifting her focus off the neglected relationship and onto their worth. He counters by falling even further away, with the result that both feel offended by the other's actions or lack thereof.

Their marriage slowly dies as they become increasingly disconnected, until they reach the breaking point when Caleb's wife tells him that she wants a divorce. This gives Caleb a reality check of the harshest kind. He's been saving other people's lives and neglecting his own. Happy families are celebrating that they have regained a loved one they thought would die, but in the meantime, Caleb is letting his marriage die. One of his colleagues brings that point home hard when he says, "The sad part about it is, when most people promise for better or for worse, they really only mean for the better."

Caleb has disconnected not only from his wife, but even more dangerously, from the Lord. His inflated ego has gotten in his way. Because he's a "hero" to his friends and the community, it's easy for him to believe that he's not at fault. He follows that line of thinking to its logical (but wrong) conclusion that since it's not his fault, he doesn't have to do anything in the relationship—other than become angry.

Caleb needs to realize that he has two relationships to mend: one with God and one with his wife. And they need to be mended in a specific order. There's no way his marriage can be resurrected and begin to flourish without the Lord's hand guiding him and his wife out of the valley of dry bones.

Once Caleb understands that he hasn't been loving his wife the way God instructed him to do, that he has been selfish, the couple is able to take the first steps on the long, difficult path out of that dark place.

The superhero movie *Doctor Strange* states this in a poignant way when the Ancient One, who is mentoring Doctor Stephen Strange, is dying and has a quiet conversation with the hero. She's trying to encourage him, but he's resistant. She finally says, "Arrogance and fear still keep you from learning the simplest and most significant lesson of all."[21]

Strange doesn't seem convinced. If anything, he's more distraught. He counters, "Which is?"

The Ancient One looks at him, her expression filled with compassion, and says, "It's not about you."

Caleb in *Fireproof* had to learn this lesson, and all couples whose marriages are dying must take it to heart. When looking to the Lord to breathe life into their relationship, spouses must look at themselves and take responsibility for their actions rather than pointing out faults in the other person. Gary Chapman stated this bluntly in *The Five Love Languages*, reminding readers, "The object of love is not getting something you want but doing something for the well-being of the one you love."[22]

THE RESTORATION PROCESS

I had a client whose marriage was dying. Let's call her Sue. The first time I met with Sue, I found her frail, overwhelmed, and anxious. She told me that she had tried counseling in the past with no success but was adamant that the reason for the failure was that her husband was a liar. She said that she was at the end of her rope, doing everything and putting up with his lying. When Sue said "everything," she meant *everything*. She was working full time, managing the household, and dealing with three kids' school and activities.

Of course, I heard the blame right away. She was insisting that it was all her husband's fault, but she also told me that he had a drinking problem. Sue couldn't trust him to be honest about it, even after several rehab attempts.

Our first session was a storm of emotions. She wondered how to move on from the relationship and whether that would even be okay. It was clear to me that Sue didn't want the marriage to end, but she was exhausted from being the only one putting any effort into resuscitating the relationship, in addition to keeping the everyday household and work life going. Sue was dreading the social fallout as well. What would her family say? How would their church community react? How would this impact her children? Could she justify bringing them up in a "broken home"? She was also anxious about God's view of divorce.

What Sue needed, first of all, was comfort. In situations like this, I lean on Paul's words in 1 Corinthians 14:3: "But the one who prophesies speaks to people for their strengthening, encouraging and comfort" (NIV). We started our work together with this approach. It was my role to offer Sue a safe place and to speak into her so she would be strengthened, encouraged, and comforted as she shared her emotional wounds.

The next several weeks were rough. Sue did not want to be there and did not want to talk, yet once she started, she couldn't stop talking. Even though she had started off by calling her husband a liar and throwing him to the wolves, so to speak, she kept blaming herself for the events that killed their marriage. She took responsibility for fixing everything, whether or not it was hers to fix. Sue questioned what was going on with her husband, how she could get him motivated, what else she could add to her already overscheduled day, and who would say what about her.

She had lost hope in her ability to manage everything and, most importantly, was losing her faith in God. Tellingly, Sue claimed to continue to be active in her church and to be praying every day, but she confessed that her prayers were superficial. It was my role to accept her perception of events as truth for her while, at the same time, challenging those perceptions.

The process is much like Ezekiel's prophesying to dry bones. In Sue's case, it began with educating her on her anxiety and controlling behaviors. She was initially resistant to the process and didn't want to accept these things about herself. This was ironic because she was willing to accept responsibility for everything that she saw as "wrong" in her life except for what she could actually control: her own emotions and reactions.

Together, we explored Sue's childhood, relationship patterns, and belief systems. We developed new coping skills and challenged irrational belief systems. We worked toward building resilience in giving permission for others to have their own emotions. We identified resources and connections that would keep her consistent outside of the counseling sessions.

We named the anxiety, calling it out of the darkness and into the light so we could see it for what it was and it could no longer incite division in her mind. As 2 Corinthians 10:4 tells us, "We use God's mighty weapons, not worldly weapons, to knock down the strongholds of human reasoning and to destroy false arguments" (NLT). This verse is a great reminder to all believers that we're battling against spiritual forces, not other people.

Through this process, Sue's bones started rattling and coming together. God was attaching tendons to her, making flesh come upon her, and covering her with skin (Ezekiel 37:6), yet there was still more work to do. When Ezekiel was in the valley of dry bones, God said to him, "Prophesy to the breath; prophesy, son of man, and say to it, 'This is what the Sovereign LORD says: Come, breath, from the four winds and breathe into these slain, that they may live'" (Ezekiel 37:9 NIV). Ezekiel did as he was commanded, "and breath entered them; they came to life and stood up on their feet—a vast army" (Ezekiel 37:10 NIV). God was not done with my exhausted, overwhelmed, fragile client. His breath entered her, and she rose, strong!

"I didn't know I had so many control issues and that anxiety had a hold on me," Sue told me. No one had said those things to her before. She couldn't find any hope in her situation until God breathed into her and her dry bones were refreshed.

What he breathed into me was the need to break the chains and generational curse of co-dependency, and unhealthy relationships w/ emotionally unavailable men because it felt familiar.

Through God's grace, the individual was being healed. It was time to focus on the marriage.

PURSUING A TEMPORARY, HEALING SEPARATION

This is when I called for a therapeutic separation. I know that sounds alarming, but don't think of it as preparation for a divorce. It's actually the opposite, though it is an extreme measure and perhaps a last-ditch effort to save the relationship. Honestly, most couples come to therapy after waiting too long, so something that extreme is necessary.

I see a therapeutic separation as validating the importance of the relationship because it shows that the spouses are willing to do anything to save their marriage, up to and including spending time apart. It creates a crisis point in the relationship because—as I say often—you can't have a miracle without a crisis.

The separation also has practical advantages. It brings relief from toxic conflict and chaos in the relationship, like a time-out between two fighting parties. It also provides an opportunity to dismantle destructive patterns of communication and brings awareness to how easy it is to take advantage of the other person or be taken advantage of in a marriage. The couple comes to understand the need for boundaries so both people can improve their coping skills and become stronger as individuals, with the goal of reuniting as a stronger couple.

In Sue's case, I had not met her husband—let's call him Simon—but she kept insisting that the marriage was worth saving. She believed that's what God was telling her, so you can understand why the idea of a therapeutic separation alarmed her. She wasn't alone. I've known other therapists and pastors to argue against the idea, wondering how any Christian therapist could advocate such a measure. My response is that Jesus regularly separated Himself from the people He loved the most, His followers and those who believed in God's Word. He spent time away from His bride to maintain and strengthen His connection to the Father.

I spoke to Sue about the idea of the Lazarus marriage, a marriage that God calls out of the grave. At this point, her marriage was in the grave. When we read the account of Lazarus in the Gospel of John, we learn that Jesus did not go to Lazarus when Lazarus was sick. He kept Himself separate until the right moment. Jesus had left Judea, where some Jews had tried to stone Him for blasphemy (John 10:29–39), and was with His disciples when He received word from Lazarus's sisters to come because "the one you love is sick" (John 11:3 NIV).

When Jesus heard this news, He said, "This sickness will not end in death. No, it is for God's glory so that God's Son may be glorified through it" (John 11:4 NIV). Even though He loved Lazarus and his two sisters, Jesus waited two more days before saying to His disciples, "Let us go back to Judea" (John 11:5–7 NIV).

His disciples were confused and tried to talk Him out of going back. They reminded Him that Judea was a place where people had tried to stone Him, as if Jesus didn't remember.

Jesus tried to explain to His disciples what was about to happen, but they weren't getting it. Finally, He spelled it out for them: "Lazarus is dead, and for your sake I am glad I was not there, so that you may believe. But let us go to him" (John 11:14–15 NIV). Thomas spoke up and rallied the others by saying, "Let us also go, that we may die with him" (John 11:16 NIV).

When Jesus arrived, Lazarus had already been in the tomb for four days. Martha approached Him and said, "Lord, ... if you had been here, my brother would not have died" (John 11:21 NIV). There's a hidden question there, perhaps even a hint of an accusation. I know that Martha gets a bad rap for her previous interaction with Jesus, in which Mary was held up as the sister who made the better choice (Luke 10:38–42), but I really want to be a Martha. She wasn't afraid to approach Jesus with questions. She complained about having to do all the work while Mary was sitting at Jesus' feet. She actually complained to the Son of God! If that isn't boldness, I'm not sure what is.

After Lazarus died, Martha was the one who met Jesus on the road while Mary stayed home (John 11:20). The roles were somewhat reversed in this case, as Mary might have been tending to the people who had come to comfort the sisters. Martha was still not afraid to question Jesus. However, she had learned from her previous interaction that the place to be was with Jesus. He had told her that the most important thing was to be with Him (Luke 10:41–42), and she did just that by going to meet Him on the road. Then Jesus called Lazarus out of the grave, from death to life, and He can call a marriage in the same way.

My client Sue and I talked about the important work that

needed to be done during a separation if the marriage was going to be brought back from the dead. She and Simon wouldn't simply go their own ways for a while, living the single life. No, a therapeutic separation requires ongoing work on the part of both spouses.

It'll Get Worse Before It Gets Better

Extreme care must be exercised in undertaking a therapeutic separation. Often one partner in the marriage is more committed than the other, even though both want to give it a shot. You have to outline the specifics of what the separation will look like. Is one person moving out? Are they maintaining separate rooms in the same house? What are they doing with each other on a weekly basis? What aspects of their early relationship will they incorporate?

In addition, I talked with Sue about how to communicate her emotions. We all know how to use words, but fewer of us know the best ways to describe our emotions, which jams us up when it comes to communicating properly. Part of that process is helping couples to understand the fight-or-flight reaction we experience in stressful situations. Another aspect is the reexamination of expectations to determine which are realistic and which are not.

I tell couples that the process is hard, and sometimes it gets worse before it gets better. That's true of therapy in general. Both spouses need to become stronger as individuals before they can save the marriage.

Part of the counseling approach with Sue involved recommending that Simon take a different approach from the therapy he was already undergoing. He needed a Christian-based approach that focused on underlying issues of sin and responsibility avoidance. To further complicate matters, Simon had started drinking again. He went into rehab for a second time, with the promise that it would never happen again.

When Simon returned home, he decided to get serious with God. He met with a counselor colleague of mine who has a powerful faith, and through this process, the Lord breathed life into Simon's dry bones. That's not to say that it was an easy journey. Simon had to rebuild trust with his wife, his children, his in-laws, and the community.

This led to trouble for Sue, at first, because her parents were bitter and angry toward Simon, so her relationship with them turned rocky. But Sue stood firmly on what God had told her: that her marriage would be restored. I like to compare this part of the process to the muscles and tendons coming back together—not just hers, but Simon's and the family's as well. I remember saying to Sue that her journey would be a great testimony they would one day use to help other couples.

I'm happy to say, with all praise to the Lord, that it came to pass. Sue and Simon are together and are mighty warriors in the kingdom of God as they minister to others. They had to work off the stink of the grave clothes, like Lazarus did. And like those skeletons in the valley of dry bones, they had to learn how to use their bodies again after being dead. They also had to recognize the difficulty others had with their new life.

People all around them were telling them not to go back and were speaking relationship death into their marriage. Those naysayers were telling them, "It's been too long. Your marriage can't be resurrected," just like the doubters told Christ that Lazarus was too far gone. Sue and Simon even said that to themselves on occasion. But the Lord said differently.

When the marriage was called out of the grave, there were people standing around, waiting for the other shoe to drop. Some even attempted to sabotage their newly revived marriage. If it sounds like what the chief priests and the Pharisees did to Jesus, yes, there is a stark similarity. They became anxious when they learned about the resurrection of Lazarus, and they began plotting to kill Jesus (John 11:46–53). At that point, God's Word tells us that "Jesus no longer moved about publicly among the people of Judea. Instead he withdrew to a region near the wilderness, to a village called Ephraim, where he stayed with his disciples" (John 11:54 NIV).

Christ had to separate Himself, and so did my client and her husband. They were called out of the marriage grave and had to set themselves apart from others and learn to work together. Then it was time for them to present themselves as united and walk in the way of the Lord.

You Get Out of Marriage What You Put Into It

The old saying that "you can't fly like an eagle if you are surrounded by turkeys" comes to mind. When we're in a difficult, disconnected relationship, we may think that it would be easier to leave the nest, fly away, and never see our partner again. As human beings, we tend to want to avoid pain. However, while it's tough to breathe new life into the dry bones of a dying marriage, there's even more pain when one ends. If both people in a couple are committed to staying in the marriage, there's a real chance for them to soar like eagles together.

The hardest part is contending with the desire for everything to be about us. We're taught from childhood how to talk and make our wants known. But as believers, we need to understand that our lives and relationships are not about us, but about being who Christ says we are. Francis Chan observed in *You and Me Forever*, "Arguments escalate when we want to be right more than we want to be *Christ*. It's easy to get blinded in the heat of disagreement. Soon, all we want is to win. Even if victory requires sin. The one who wins the argument is usually the one who acts *less* like Christ."[23]

We need to come to terms with what's actually within our control and work from there to make changes. We cannot make someone feel a particular emotion, but we can invite, influence, impact, and trigger that person's emotions. Gary Chapman gave the example of a husband who walks into the house and doesn't even attempt to connect with his wife. Instead, he reaches for the TV remote, talks to the dog, and goes about getting something to eat before bothering to check in with her.[24]

You can see how, over time, this behavior will crush her spirit. As King Solomon said in Proverbs 17:22, "A cheerful heart is good medicine, but a crushed spirit dries up the bones" (NIV). Once again, this is the case of one person being ignorant of the other's needs and focusing only on his own. That kind of attitude is the doom of a functional, loving marriage.

The simple truth is that you will get out of a marriage what you put into it. Successfully reviving a Lazarus marriage means understanding your emotions and making sure that your expectations are realistic. As you learn more about yourself and become healthier and stronger as an individual, your needs and purposes will change, and how you perceive your spouse and his or her needs will change as well. We need to be willing to evolve in those ways and understand that the other person is doing the same. We must show our spouses the same love that Christ has for us—the selfless, sacrificial love that led Him to die for us on the cross. Only then can we bring our marriages out of the grave and fly like eagles together.

WORKBOOK

Chapter Nine Questions

Question: What challenges do you currently face in your marriage?

_____
_____
_____
_____
_____
_____
_____
_____
_____
_____
_____

Question: Without casting blame, how can you begin taking responsibility for what's actually within your control? What changes can you make to become healthier and stronger as an individual?

_____

_____

_____

_____

_____

_____

_____

_____

_____

_____

Question: Before reading this chapter, how did you view separation and its effect on a marriage? Do you view it differently now? Why or why not?

_____

_____

_____

_____
_____
_____
_____
_____
_____
_____

Action: This week, focus on truly listening to your spouse. At the end of the week, identify one need your spouse has that's going unmet. Consider specific ways you can help to meet that need and put those measures into practice. Pay attention to how the dynamics of your relationship change as you seek to show love to your spouse in this way.

Dec 1, 2023

As I struggled w/ having to communicate more regularly w/ Marc + the stress & "anguish" created by a counselor who keeps referring to show we need to "move toward" each other —

No! we don't. He is an abuser & "not" repentant & has not re- built the trust. So no! Again I began to feel that I have to control. Then tonight God "... Don't concern yourself w/ what Marc does. Just watch what I do. Eyes on Me." Suddenly

[margin:] Don't worry about what he does — wanted you to do — We + the rest of the rest of it.

Chapter Nine Notes

11/28/2023

p. 161 I don't think Marc + I did a very good job of discussing our needs or expectations + when to all the "premarital" crap.

p. 162 I'm grieving the death/loss of the relationship I had w/ my "friend" + playmate Marc + the idea of taking care of each other.

At this point it would take a miracle —

I see nothing in Marc that indicates love or truth — I see more hiding, lying, faking it. → His words are what he Thinks I want to hear but his actions do **NOT** match his words.

I been blaming others and making excuses for his volatility, explosiveness + verbal abuse.

p. 163 Marc listens to the enemy + does it even recognize the lies.

*Marc's other relationships didn't see the violence because they didn't stick around long enough. My guess is that

> When they began to express their needs, it wasn't just @ Marc getting what he wanted — they had to go & be kicked then out of "this house -"
>
> p. 168 What "spiritual" battles am I fighting where Marc & I are concerned?

CHAPTER TEN

Hope in the Lord

There is a little country church not far down the road. It looks like it should be featured on a greeting card. The building is brick and has a tall steeple with a cross that spans the roof. It's very quaint and devoid of the contemporary worship dressings. When I ride by this church, it instills in me a sense of reverence.

The church is surrounded by a graveyard, as the older places of worship often are. I'm reminded of the generations that have been a part of that church and helped to establish it in the community. This takes me to a place of romanticizing about how a small but mighty country church came to be and passed the test of time. I wonder if the founders knew the impact they would have on the kingdom of God. I wonder if those who came after and those who are still there realize how they will impact future generations to come.

The romanticizing stops when I remember the present-day reality of that church. People who, in the name of Jesus, allowed their egos to get in the way of ministry caused years of division. They forgot the call of the country church and sought to keep the focus on their own needs. The congregation dwindled, and their impact on the community diminished.

Now more tombstones mark the resting place of dearly departed saints than parking spaces herald the arrival of the few living saints who still attend. It's not only surrounded by the physical dry bones of believers awaiting the resurrection, but also filled with the dry bones of those who are sitting in the pews.

Man Sees the Outside, But God Sees the Inside

This little country church surrounded by graves shows how the outside may reflect what's happening on the inside: dry bones inside and out. The grass around the building and the graves is manicured, indicating some level of care. The members seem attentive to the upkeep of the building, at least externally. But what about the attendees on the inside? What about the condition of their hearts?

Jesus upbraided the Pharisees, saying, "Woe to you, teachers of the law and Pharisees, you hypocrites! You clean the outside of the cup and dish, but inside they are full of greed and self-indulgence" (Matthew 23:25 NIV). He then chastised their obsession with hiding what's really going on inside, adding, "Woe to you, teachers of the law and Pharisees, you hypocrites! You are like whitewashed tombs, which look beautiful on the outside but on the inside are full of the bones of the dead and everything unclean" (Matthew 23:27 NIV).

It sounds gloomy, but there is hope, as we've seen throughout the other chapters spent grappling with real and powerful emotions. It may be tempting to give up and say, "I can't do this," or "Nothing's ever going to change, so why bother?" But that simply isn't true. Our God is not a god of dismay and despair. He offers us the ultimate hope in salvation and, while we're here on the earth, allows us to put our hope in Him so we can shine in the darkest circumstances. His is the voice crying out in the wilderness, prophesying into the valley of dry bones, so that we're put back together, piece by piece.

What steps do we need to take to walk out of the valley of dry bones and embrace the new life that God offers? Anne Frank wrote in her *Diary of a Young Girl*, "Where there's hope, there's life. It fills us with fresh courage and makes us strong again."

CULTIVATING EMOTIONAL RESILIENCE

The key to inner strength is building emotional resilience, the ability to respond to stressful, unexpected situations or crises and adapt in a flexible manner to those events. Building resilience is not easy or immediate.

The Lord breathed new life into the dry bones, but His restoration of the bodies wasn't an instant fix. There was a process involved. Muscle and sinew had to be attached to the bones before they could be of use again, and God had to breathe into them before they could be fully alive.

God can and will deliver us from the bondage of emotions that keep us disconnected from ourselves, our loved ones, and our community. We need to have hope, patience, and perseverance for the process. Once we're recovering, we must put in place mechanisms that will help to prevent us from returning to that dark valley.

Do you yawn and stretch when you first wake up? There's a term for that: *pandiculating*. It's the involuntary response to a lack of movement and the tension built up in our muscles. According to science educator Luis Villazon, "When you sleep, your muscles lose tone and fluid tends to pool along your back. Stretching helps to massage fluid gently back into the normal position. Also, your muscles protect themselves from over-extension by inhibiting the nerve impulses as they approach their limit." [25] The act of pandiculating is an innate, healthy behavior. It differs from voluntary stretching in that it involves the brain's understanding of the muscles. Pandiculation is contracting the muscles and then slowly releasing, actively using the muscles in order to affect change from the inside out. That's what we have to do. We have to get ourselves up and get used to walking in a new normal.

Think back to our discussions of anxiety and anger, which are triggered from primary emotions. It's like we have inside us all of these generals issuing orders and troops responding, causing our minds and bodies to react in certain ways. Once we learn how to process those emotions properly, we can pause the fight-or-flight response and determine if the threat is real or perceived.

This is where having an attitude of gratitude comes into play. We can be grateful that our bodies respond to threats, either real or perceived. It's up to us to handle the information in the correct way. If it's a perceived threat, we can employ strategies to deal with the anger and anxiety rather than giving in to them and letting them give the orders. This helps us to understand and be less triggered by those emotions the next time they pop up.

ANXIETY AND HOPE

There's a lot of debate when it comes to the "thorn" given to the Apostle Paul so he would not become arrogant (2 Corinthians 12:7). Some think it was a physical handicap or malady, but I suggest that it was anxiety. Anxiety has proven to be crippling for many people across the centuries, and we see evidence of it where Paul wrote, "Therefore I am all the more eager to send him, so that when you see him again you may be glad and I may have less anxiety" (Philippians 2:28 NIV).

There's a common saying that "those who can't do teach." In other words, those who teach know the material but cannot apply the material to their lives. This is unflattering to teachers, and though I don't believe it to be true, I do believe that we tend to focus on what we know. When I know something, I can teach and write about it. Paul knew anxiety, I think, so he wrote about it. Again, what I love about Paul is that he didn't leave it there. He didn't allow himself to stay in the valley of dry bones; he provided hope for the future.

Let's flip back further in Scripture to find another person of faith who had anxiety: Daniel. Did I say Daniel, the one from the well-known story of being trapped in the lion's den? Yes, one and the same.

It surprises me, too. After all, Daniel stood up to the culture and the king, faced death by lions, and survived without so much as a tooth mark or a claw's scratch (Daniel 6). And yet, the reactions recorded in chapter 10 were not those of an inwardly brave and bold man: "I had no strength left, my face turned deathly pale and I was helpless" (Daniel 10:8 NIV), and "A hand touched me and set me trembling on my hands and knees" (Daniel 10:10 NIV).

Daniel was told not to be afraid, but he said, "I am overcome with anguish because of the vision, my lord, and I feel very weak. How can I, your servant, talk with you, my lord? My strength is gone and I can hardly breathe" (Daniel 10:16–17 NIV). It sounds like Daniel was having a panic attack.

Why bring up Paul's and Daniel's struggles when we're supposed to be talking about hope? We tend to place the great people of faith in the Bible on lofty pedestals, and it's beneficial for us to remember that they, too, sometimes had to climb out of the valley of dry bones. The emotions they wrestled with millennia ago were no different from what we all deal with today. It's encouraging to realize that these biblical figures were people just like us, with their own traumas and difficulties. God provided them with hope and healing, as He will do for us.

James was clear about what we would face in his letter to the believers. He wrote, "Consider it pure joy, my brothers and sisters, whenever you face trials of many kinds, because you know that the testing of your faith produces perseverance. Let perseverance finish its work so that you may be mature and complete, not lacking anything" (James 1:2–4 NIV).

The more you trust God as you go through trials and hardships, the more you build your faith. Your emotional resilience and ability to manage stressful events and circumstances come from your belief that there's more to life than the here and now; there's a there and then. The "then" is eternal rather than internal. You start asking questions beyond what's going on with you. What does God want? What is His plan for you? It feels good and safe to rely on your heavenly Father, and the more you adopt an eternal perspective, the better you get at it.

HOPE IN THE VALLEY OF DRY BONES

- Remember that the valley of dry bones is not a place you're meant to remain forever. It's also not a place you can leave without help and work. You must be willing to allow someone to prophesy to you. As you travel across the wastes, you need to be aware of what God is asking you to do. You need to be diligent and intentional about doing those things, because that will help you to hold on to the knowledge that God is working in and through you. He is not finished with you yet.

When I was in my own valley of dry bones, I didn't want to do the work. I didn't want to pray. I didn't want to do the Bible studies. I didn't want to examine my emotions and my reactions. Still, I knew that God would use those things to lead me out of the valley, so I committed to doing the work in a more coherent, compassionate manner, rather than letting the good habits I had die.

As you become more aware of yourself, you will see what God is leading you to step out and tackle, and you'll begin doing the work that builds your emotional resilience. Self-awareness is key. After all, you can't change what you don't acknowledge.

As difficult as it may seem, keep in mind that God is always up to something. He is working for your good and His purposes in all kinds of struggles and difficulties. "One of life's strategic keys is learning to embrace what our Lord brings into our lives with thanksgiving," Darien B. Cooper wrote in her devotional for *Hinds' Feet on High Places*. "When we do so, we recognize His sovereign control and completely yield ourselves to Him. He will never waste our sorrows. On the contrary, He turns them into precious jewels! As for our suffering, He uses it to birth beautiful new things into our lives. So if we keep these things in mind, it makes the pain more bearable and it seems less senseless."[26]

Making sense of the seemingly senseless goes a long way toward calming our jangled nerves. This brings us back around to purpose. Everyone searches for purpose and meaning in life. Who better than the Lord to show us what that purpose is? He shines His light to direct us on the path out of the valley of dry bones and onto fertile plains that are ripe with possibilities.

How can we move ahead on this path if we're so often mired in the past? Our cares and worries pile up like those sharp-edged, desiccated bones, making it impossible for us to step free. Paul urged us to direct our minds toward positive thoughts: "Finally, brothers and sisters, whatever is true, whatever is noble, whatever is right, whatever is pure, whatever is lovely, whatever is admirable—if anything is excellent or praiseworthy—think about such things" (Philippians 4:8 NIV). That doesn't mean ignoring our past, which is full of lessons for how we can better manage our emotions, but we can learn to accept things the way they are. Focusing on what is redirects our attention to the here and now.

LIVE IN THE PRESENT

Now breathe. Exercise that deep in and out from the depths of your body and embrace the calmness. Focus on one thing at a time. Maintain boundaries with others and also within yourself. Adjust your expectations to fit the real facts and show yourself the same compassion and appreciation you have for the people you love. Don't compare yourself to others, but rather focus on what God wants to do in your life. "Take captive every thought," as Paul told the Corinthians (2 Corinthians 10:5 NIV). Don't worry about tomorrow, because God's love for you surpasses every care (Matthew 6:25–34).

"Oh yes, the past can hurt," the wise Rafiki says in *The*

Lion King. "But you can either run from it or <u>learn from it</u>."²⁷

Oftentimes we go about our lives, waiting for the miracle that will rejuvenate our dry bones. I think of Habakkuk, who was so anxious at the danger coming his way that he wrote, "I heard and my heart pounded, my lips quivered at the sound; decay crept into my bones, and my legs trembled" (Habakkuk 3:16 NIV). This man was so terrified that he felt like he was dying.

Then Habakkuk's anxiety was swept away by the Lord's arrival: "The Sovereign LORD is my strength; he makes my feet like the feet of a deer, he enables me to tread on the heights" (Habakkuk 3:19 NIV). His words give fresh meaning to the phrase "leaping for joy."

Let's return for a moment to the dying church surrounded by acres of tombstones. From a therapist's perspective, I often find that what I see on the outside is an indicator of what's on the inside. When I see someone who seemingly has it all together, I wonder if this person is managing a high level of anxiety and a low tolerance for imperfection. Many people hold the belief that appearing perfect on the outside is the only way to feel in control and purposeful.

Individuals with this mindset are very hard on themselves for any mistake or flaw. They tend to compare themselves to other people and struggle with what others may think of them. They find validation in presenting themselves as perfect and in other people's opinions. Paul warned against this way of thinking. He wrote, "Not that we dare to classify or compare ourselves with some of those who are commending themselves. But when they measure themselves by one another and compare themselves with one another, they are without understanding" (2 Corinthians 10:12 ESV).

On the other hand, when there's a lot of disruption on the outside, such as hoarding, it gives a clue about the difficulty an individual has with letting go. It suggests finding validation in things. Jesus said, "Do not store up for yourselves treasures on earth, where moths and vermin destroy, and where thieves break in and steal. But store up for yourselves treasures in heaven, where moths and vermin do not destroy, and where thieves do not break in and steal. For where your treasure is, there your heart will be also" (Matthew 6:19–21 NIV).

There comes a time when God releases people from certain churches, like He released me and my husband from ministry. As we traveled, we were "church homeless" for a while, if you will, and went to all kinds of places and visited several different denominations. After that period of wandering, God prepared for us a new ministry back in the same denomination, though in a new church.

Sometimes I work with a client who is in the dry bones of his or her church life. Even as others are leaving that particular church, the way opens for my client to leave the valley of dry bones and thrive in that church. It's fascinating to watch the body of believers on the move. What we're seeing is God moving His people for His purposes. That's what He did with the Israelites. He moved them with purpose. When He moves you, it feels difficult. Change always is. God wants us to show up like kids—willing, open, excited, and ready to go <u>all in</u>. There's great hope in that approach to life.

In Genesis 2:7, we learn that "the LORD God formed a man from the dust of the ground and breathed into his nostrils the breath of life, and the man became a living being" (NIV). In our minds, it's a smooth, gentle breath, and then Adam came alive. God used His breath to give life and fulfill His purpose. What if the breath He uses to revive our dry bones is a hot, angry breath that gets us moving? This breath causes us to come alive and jump up, because otherwise we would stay stagnant on the valley floor.

FINDING JOY AND HOPE IN GOD'S PURPOSE

A few years ago, my husband was in a terrible accident. He was hit by a live-haul tractor-trailer truck, and the van he was driving was buried under crates of live chickens. When I tell the story, no one expects me to say that the cargo was live chickens. The rescue personnel had to use the jaws of life to free him and then a forklift to heave everything out of the way.

It was a horrific nightmare on the road, with a Flight for Life helicopter and emergency vehicles everywhere. There was a couple there who told me, "Hey, he's fine. He's alive. He's talking." I told them, with a bit of humor in the face of the trauma, "Thank you. I appreciate that. But my husband's going to be talking about ten minutes after he is gone."

I found my husband on a stretcher, covered with blood and feathers. They were loading him into an ambulance. Just

Hope in the Lord

as expected, he was talking. We joked about having chicken on the grill, even as he was being readied for a trip to the hospital. The police officer noticed this and remarked, "You're awfully calm." I agreed, and when she asked what I did for a living, I told her. She nodded and said, "So that's why you're so calm."

But that wasn't the reason. I explained to her, "No, I'm calm because I choose to see what's right about this, not what's wrong. I choose to see that he had the ability to tell someone else my cell phone number without having to punch it up on his phone. All this other stuff is, well, other stuff." *Let the "other stuff" go — be free!*

That's how resilience building enables us to respond. If we always look at what's wrong, then we miss out on what's right. We should ask ourselves what God wants out of this particular event, situation, or crisis. We can't have a miracle without a crisis. We all want miracles, but none of us want crises. We can find joy and peace if we focus on what Paul wrote to the Philippians:

> *Rejoice in the Lord always. I will say it again: Rejoice! Let your gentleness be evident to all. The Lord is near. Do not be anxious about <u>anything</u>, but in <u>every situation</u>, by prayer and petition, with thanksgiving, present your requests to God. And the peace of God, which transcends all understanding, will guard your hearts and your minds in Christ Jesus.*
> —***Philippians 4:4–7*** *(NIV)*

My husband leaned into that hope. There were things he wasn't able to do after his accident, limitations that were placed upon him, but he didn't dwell on that. He chose to let the Lord lead him away from the valley of dry bones. He chose to learn, as Paul did, "to be content whatever the circumstances" (Philippians 4:11–13 NIV). This takes practice and consistent prayer because it doesn't come naturally. We need God to increase our understanding and to build emotional resilience in our hearts and minds.

Whatever you face, keep an eternal perspective. Never let yourself forget that God has a purpose for you. This will hold you close to the Lord as He reaches out His hand, reconnecting your bones and stretching out those tendons, and breathes life into what was dead.

Do you hear that rattling? It's perfectly normal. It's the sound of your new life beginning. It's the sound of heavenly hope. *Praise him!*

WORKBOOK

Chapter Ten Questions

Question: In what ways might God want to use a difficult circumstance to build your emotional resilience? What work do you need to do to allow this to happen?

- Boundaries w/ parents.
- 100% responsibility for MY life
- Walking ourendly on the path he's laid out for me.
- Keep + develop my ETERNAL perspective.
- Do the work
- Receive his JOY

Question: What difference would hope make in your life?

All the difference! Hope leads me forward, hope leads "into" great. Hope brings & releases Joy

Question: Where can you find hope if you're in the valley of dry bones?

Counselling, my new business, serving the west, seeing all that he's doing in my life + my friends lives.

_____
_____
_____
_____

Action: The next time you feel anxious or angry, take a moment to breathe slowly in and out. Feel the calmness returning to your mind and body. Now focus on the present moment. What negative thoughts are you having toward yourself and others? Are they based on truth or on unrealistic expectations? Replace the negative thoughts with positive ones full of Christ's love and compassion for you and other people. How does your view of the situation change? Go through this process each time you find yourself in a stressful situation until it becomes second nature to you.

[Handwritten margin note: God's plans & purpose.]

[Handwritten note: Breathe & see God's purpose. Lay down my tracks - getting there, enjoying the journey.]

Chapter Ten Notes

p.184 - Strategies to re-engage w/ myself - Reconnect w/ running community + racing (5K).

Coach myself - I am a good coach

p.185 - My anxiety over having to talk w/ Marc is a "perceived" threat. I have a powerful loving father + I have protections in place to keep myself safe from him. I never have to live with him again if I am not safe + loved - He has a lot of work to do for that to happen.

p.184 - Walking in my "new normal" requires me to take 100% responsibility for my life + my responsibilities first.

12/9/2023 So today when I call my mom @ coming to N.C. - I'm coming in January to avoid holiday traffic - my safety + enjoyment of the trip + to get the good work hours I need - (2) new clients.

what "primary" emotions trouble me the most?

About the Author

Patricia Boyce is a Licensed Professional Counselor of Mental Health in Delaware and Maryland. She is Nationally Certified, with a master's degree in counseling and a doctorate in psychology. She has been in private practice since 2003, having previously worked in the private and government sectors. In 2003, she received the Presidential Leadership Award.

Patricia loves to mentor entrepreneurs, interns, and doctoral students. She sees individuals with concerns related to adjustment, anxiety, anger, depression, domestic violence, and grief, among others.

Patricia has been with her husband for decades. She enjoys two sons and many (great-)grandchildren.

Acknowledgments

I did not "show up" here all on my own, so there are many people I must acknowledge. But first and foremost, I acknowledge God, who through His Holy Spirit and Son enables me to be the humble vessel for others' pain.

I thank my husband for his unconditional support and love. He has said that I "got my best training right there at home," and I am grateful for that on-the-job training. Thank you for all the years of laughter and love!

Thanks also to my family, who have expressed their love in so many ways. You warm my heart and I am so proud of each and every one of you.

Thank you to my mother for putting me on the Sunday school bus as a little girl. You have encouraged me in so many ways to be a strong, critically thinking woman.

I thank my brother for his strength and tenacity. You have been an example of how, even though life gets in the way, you just keep moving.

To my amazing friend Donna: thank you for being such a good friend. You help me to be a better person.

Thank you to author Leslie Dean for being a writing inspiration. Your story has helped so many others find hope, and I pray this one does, too.

I also owe thanks to the Bible study ladies, who keep me accountable to being authentic and vulnerable. You have been so faithful in exploring God's word!

I want to acknowledge and thank my therapist colleagues who are walking with others through the Dry Bone Valley. You inspire me to be a better therapist.

And heartfelt thanks to the wonderful team who supported the words I penned, challenged me to think differently, and edited, formatted, and prepared this final project. You have been the ones who held the light for me as I traveled through this process.

About Renown Publishing

Renown Publishing is the proud publishing imprint of Speak It To Book, an elite team of publishing professionals devoted to helping you shape, write, and share your book. Renown has written, edited, and worked on hundreds of books (including New York Times, Wall Street Journal, and USA Today best-sellers, and the #1 book on all of Amazon).

We believe authentic stories are the torch of change-makers, and our mission is to collaborate with purpose-driven authors to create societal impact and redeem culture.

If you're the founder of a purpose-driven company, visit RenownPublishing.com.

If you're an aspiring author, visit SpeakItToBook.com.

REFERENCES

Notes

[1] Black, Claudia. *It Will Never Happen to Me*. M.A.C., 1982.

[2] Carder, Dave, Earl Henslin, John Townsend, Henry Cloud, and Alice Brawand. *Secrets of Your Family Tree: Healing for Adult Children of Dysfunctional Families*. New edition. Moody, 1995, p. 131.

[3] Black, Claudia. *Changing Course: Healing from Loss, Abandonment, and Fear*. 3rd edition. Central Recovery Press, 2021.

[4] Allers, Roger, and Rob Minkoff, dirs. *The Lion King*. Buena Vista Pictures, 1994.

[5] Black, *Changing Course*, p. 17.

[6] Nay, W. Robert. *Taking Charge of Anger*. Guilford Press, 2012.

[7] Frankel, David, dir. *Hope Springs*. Sony Pictures, 2012.

[8] Plato. *Charmides*. Translated by Benjamin Jowett. 1892.

[9] Blue Letter Bible, "Strong's G964 –*bēthesda*." https://www.blueletterbible.org/lexicon/g964/esv/mgnt/0-1/.

[10] Amen, Daniel. "Do You Have an ANT Infestation in Your Head?" Amen Clinics. September 16, 2020.

https://www.amenclinics.com/blog/do-you-have-an-ant-infestation-in-your-head/.

[11] Kübler-Ross, Elisabeth. *On Death and Dying*. Macmillan, 1969.

[12] Kübler-Ross, *On Death and Dying*.

[13] Avildsen, John G., dir. *The Karate Kid*. Columbia Pictures, 1984.

[14] Hirschman, R. S., and M. A. Safer. "Hemisphere Differences in Perceiving Positive and Negative Emotions." *Cortex* 18, no. 4 (December 1982): p. 569–580.

[15] Clinton, Tim, and Gary Sibcy. *Why You Do the Things You Do*. Thomas Nelson, 2006, p. 21.

[16] Clinton and Sibcy, *Why You Do the Things You Do*, p. 51.

[17] Dean, Leslie T. *Forgiven Much*. Xulon Press, 2006, p. 92.

[18] Chapman, Gary. *The Five Love Languages*. Northfield Publishing, 1992.

[19] Docter, Pete, dir. *Inside Out*. Walt Disney Studios, 1995.

[20] Kendrick, Alex, dir. *Fireproof*. Affirm Films, 2008.

[21] Derrickson, Scott, dir. *Doctor Strange*. Walt Disney Studios, 2016.

[22] Chapman, *The Five Love Languages*.

[23] Chan, Francis, and Lisa Chan. *You and Me Forever: Marriage in Light of Eternity*. Claire Love Publishing, 2014.

[24] Chapman, *The Five Love Languages*.

[25] Villazon, Luis. "Why Do We Stretch When We Wake Up?" BBC Science Focus Magazine. https://www.sciencefocus.com/the-human-body/why-do-we-stretch-when-we-wake-up/.

[26] Cooper, Darien B., and Hannah Hurnard. *Hinds' Feet on High Places: The Original and Complete Allegory with a Devotional for Women*. Reissue edition. Destiny Image, 2013.

[27] Allers and Minkoff, *The Lion King*.

Made in the USA
Middletown, DE
26 October 2023

41453397R00119